SONGS OF SUMMER LANDS

SONGS OF SUMMER LANDS

By JOAQUIN MILLER,

AUTHOR OF "SONGS OF THE SIERRAS AND SUNLANDS," ETC., ETC.

where the sun and the moon lay down together and brought forth the stars.

CHICAGO

MORRILL, HIGGINS & CO.

1892.

CONTENTS.

SONGS OF SUMMER LANDS.

IN that far land, farther than Yucatan,
Hondurian height, or Mahogany steep,
Where the great sea, hollowed by the hand of man,
Hears deep come calling across to deep;
Where the great seas follow in the grooves of men
Down under the bastions of Darien:

In that land so far that you wonder whether
If God would know it should you fall down dead;
In that land so far through the wilds and weather
That the lost sun sinks like a warrior sped,—
Where the sea and the sky seem closing together,
Seem closing together as a book that is read:

In that nude, warm world, where the unnamed rivers
Roll restless in cradles of bright buried gold;
Where white flashing mountains flow rivers of silver,
As a rock of the desert flowed fountains of old;
By a dark, wooded river that calls to the dawn,
And calls all day with his dolorous swan:

In that land of the wonderful sun and weather,
With green under foot and with gold over head,
Where the spent sun flames, and you wonder whether
'Tis an isle of fire in his foamy bed:
Where the oceans of earth shall be welded together
By the great French master in his forge flame red,—

Lo! the half-finished world! Yon footfall retreating,—
It might be the Maker disturbed at his task.
But the footfall of God, or the far pheasant beating,
It is one and the same, whatever the mask
It may wear unto man. The woods keep repeating
The old sacred sermons, whatever you ask.

It is man in his garden, scarce wakened as yet
From the sleep that fell on him when woman was made.
The new-finished garden is plastic and wet
From the hand that has fashioned its unpeopled shade;
And the wonder still looks from the fair woman's eyes
As she shines through the wood like the light from the skies.

And a ship now and then from some far Ophir's shore
Draws in from the sea. It lies close to the bank;
Then a dull, muffled sound of the slow shuffled plank
As they load the black ship; but you hear nothing more,
And the dark, dewy vines, and the tall, sombre wood
Like twilight droop over the deep, sweeping flood.

The black masts are tangled with branches that cross,
The rich, fragrant gums fall from branches to deck,

The thin ropes are swinging with streamers of moss
That mantle all things like the shreds of a wreck;
The long mosses swing, there is never a breath:
The river rolls still as the river of death.

THE SEA OF FIRE.

I.

In the beginning,—ay, before
The six-days' labors were well o'er;
Yea, while the world lay incomplete,
Ere God had opened quite the door
Of this strange land for strong men's feet,—
There lay against that westmost sea
One weird-wild land of mystery.

A far white wall, like fallen moon,
Girt out the world. The forest lay
So deep you scarcely saw the day,
Save in the high-held middle noon:
It lay a land of sleep and dreams,
And clouds drew through like shoreless streams
That stretch to where no man may say.

Men reached it only from the sea,
By black-built ships, that seemed to creep
Along the shore suspiciously,
Like unnamed monsters of the deep.
It was the weirdest land, I ween,
That mortal eye has ever seen:

A dim, dark land of bird and beast,
Black shaggy beasts with cloven claw,—
A land that scarce knew prayer or priest,
Or law of man, or Nature's law;
Where no fixed line drew sharp dispute
'Twixt savage man and silent brute.

II.

It hath a history most fit
For cunning hand to fashion on;
No chronicler hath mentioned it;
No buccaneer set foot upon.
'Tis of an outlawed Spanish Don,—
A cruel man, with pirate's gold
That loaded down his deep ship's hold.

A deep ship's hold of plundered gold!
The golden cruise, the golden cross,
From many a church of Mexico,
From Panama's mad overthrow,
From many a ransomed city's loss,
From many a follower stanch and bold,
And many a foeman stark and cold.

He found this wild, lost land. He drew
His ship to shore. His ruthless crew,
Like Romulus, laid lawless hand
On meek brown maidens of the land,
And in their bloody forays bore
Red firebrands along the shore.

III.

The red men rose at night. They came,
A firm, unflinching wall of flame;
They swept, as sweeps some fateful sea
O'er land of sand and level shore
That howls in far, fierce agony.
The red men swept that deep, dark shore
As threshers sweep a threshing floor.

And yet beside the slain Don's door
They left his daughter, as they fled:
They spared her life because she bore
Their Chieftain's blood and name. The red
And blood-stained hidden hoards of gold
They hollowed from the stout ship's hold,
And bore in many a slim canoe—
To where? The good priest only knew.

IV.

The course of life is like the sea;
Men come and go; tides rise and fall;
And that is all of history.
The tide flows in, flows out to-day—
And that is all that man may say;
Man is, man was,—and that is all.

Revenge at last came like a tide,—
'T was sweeping deep and terrible;
The Christian found the land, and came
To take possession in Christ's name.
For every white man tha thad died
I think a thousand red men fell,—

A Christian custom; and the land
Lay lifeless as some burned-out brand.

V.

Ere while the slain Don's daughter grew
A glorious thing, a flower of spring,
A lithe slim reed, a sun-loved weed,
A something more than mortal knew;
A mystery of grace and face,—
A silent mystery that stood
An empress in that sea-set wood,
Supreme, imperial in her place.

It might have been men's lust for gold,—
For all men knew that lawless crew
Left hoards of gold in that ship's hold,
That drew ships hence, and silent drew
Strange Jasons to that steep wood shore,
As if to seek that hidden store,—
I never either cared or knew.

I say it might have been this gold
That ever drew and strangely drew

Strong men of land, strange men of sea,
To seek this shore of mystery
With all its wondrous tales untold;
The gold or her, which of the two?
It matters not; I never knew.

But this I know, that as for me,
Between that face and the hard fate
That kept me ever from my own,
As some wronged monarch from his throne,
God's heaped-up gold of land or sea
Had never weighed one feather's weight.

Her home was on the wooded height,—
A woody home, a priest at prayer,
A perfume in the fervid air,
And angels watching her at night.
I can but think upon the skies
That bound that other Paradise.

VI.

Below a star-built arch, as grand
As ever bended heaven spanned;

Tall trees like mighty columns grew—
They loomed as if to pierce the blue,
They reached as reaching heaven through.

The shadowed stream rolled far below,
Where men moved noiseless to and fro
As in some vast cathedral, when
The calm of prayer comes to men,
With benedictions, bending low.

Lo! wooded sea-banks, wild and steep!
A trackless wood; a snowy cone
That lifted from this wood alone!
This wild, wide river, dark and deep!
A ship against the shore asleep!

VII.

An Indian woman crept, a crone,
Hard by about the land alone,
The relic of her perished race.
She wore rich, rudely-fashioned bands
Of gold above her bony hands:
She hissed hot curses on the place!

VIII.

Go seek the red man's last retreat!
A lonesome land, the haunted lands!
Red mouths of beasts, red men's red hands:
Red prophet-priest, in mute defeat!

His boundaries in blood are writ!
His land is ghostland! That is his,
Whatever man may claim of this;
Beware how you shall enter it!
He stands God's guardian of ghostlands;
Ay, this same wrapped half-prophet stands
All nude and voiceless, nearer to
The awful God than I or you.

IX.

This bronzed child, by that river's brink,
Stood fair to see as you can think,
As tall as tall reeds at her feet,
As fresh as flowers in her hair;
As sweet as flowers over-sweet,
As fair as vision more than fair!

How beautiful she was! How wild!
How pure as water-plant, this child,—
This one wild child of Nature here
Grown tall in shadows.
                                        And how near
To God, where no man stood between
Her eyes and scenes no man hath seen,—
This maiden that so mutely stood,
The one lone woman of that wood.

Stop still, my friend, and do not stir,
Shut close your page and think of her.
The birds sang sweeter for her face;
Her lifted eyes were like a grace
To seamen of that solitude,
However rough, however rude.

The rippled rivers of her hair,
That ran in wondrous waves, somehow
Flowed down divided by her brow,—
Half mantled her within its care,
And flooded all, or bronze or snow,
In its uncommon fold and flow.

A perfume and an incense lay
Before her, as an incense sweet

Before blithe mowers of sweet May
In early morn. Her certain feet
Embarked on no uncertain way.

Come, think how perfect before men,
How sweet as sweet magnolia bloom
Embalmed in dews of morning, when
Rich sunlight leaps from midnight gloom
Resolved to kiss, and swift to kiss
Ere yet morn wakens man to bliss.

X.

The days swept on. Her perfect year
Was with her now. The sweet perfume
Of womanhood in holy bloom,
As when red harvest blooms appear,
Possessed her now. The priest did pray
That saints alone should pass that way.

A red bird built beneath her roof,
Brown squirrels crossed her cabin sill,
And welcome came or went at will.
A hermit spider wove his web,

And up against the roof would spin
His net to catch mosquitoes in.

The silly elk, the spotted fawn,
And all dumb beasts that came to drink,
That stealthy stole upon the brink
In that dim while that lies between
The coming night and going dawn,
On seeing her familiar face
Would fearless stop and stand in place.

She was so kind, the beasts of night
Gave her the road as if her right;
The panther crouching overhead
In sheen of moss would hear her tread,
And bend his eyes, but never stir
Lest he by chance might frighten her.

Yet in her splendid strength, her eyes,
There lay the lightning of the skies;
The love-hate of the lioness,
To kill the instant or caress:
A pent-up soul that sometimes grew
Impatient; why, she hardly knew.

At last she sighed, uprose, and threw
Her strong arms out as if to hand
Her love, sun-born and all complete
At birth, to some brave lover's feet
On some far, fair, and unseen land,
As knowing now not what to do!

XI.

How beautiful she was! Why, she
Was inspiration! She was born
To walk God's summer hills at morn,
Nor waste her by this wood-dark sea.
What wonder, then, her soul's white wings
Beat at its bars, like living things!

Once more she sighed! She wandered
through
The sea-bound wood, then stopped and
drew
Her hand above her face, and swept
The lonesome sea, and all day kept
Her face to sea, as if she knew
Some day, some near or distant day,
Her destiny should come that way.

XII.

How proud she was! How darkly fair!
How full of faith, of love; of strength!
Her calm, proud eyes! Her great hair's
length,—
Her long, strong, tumbled, careless hair,
Half curled and knotted anywhere,
From brow to breast, from cheek to chin,
For love to trip and tangle in!

XIII.

At last a tall strange sail was seen:
It came so slow, so wearily,
Came creeping cautious up the sea,
As if it crept from out between
The half-closed sea and sky that lay
Tight wedged together, far away.

She watched it, wooed it. She did pray
It might not pass her by but bring
Some love, some hate, some anything,

To break the awful loneliness
That like a nightly nightmare lay
Upon her proud and pent-up soul
Until it barely brooked control.

XIV.

The ship crept silent up the sea,
And came—
You cannot understand
How fair she was, how sudden she
Had sprung, full-grown, to womanhood:
How gracious, yet how proud and grand;
How glorified, yet fresh and free,
How human, yet how more than good.

XV.

The ship stole slowly, slowly on;—
Should you in Californian field
In ample flower-time behold
The soft south rose lift like a shield
Against the sudden sun at dawn,

A double handful of heaped gold,
Why you, perhaps, might understand
How splendid and how queenly she
Uprose beside that wood-set sea.

The storm-worn ship scarce seemed to creep
From wave to wave. It scarce could keep—
How still this fair girl stood, how fair!
How proud her presence as she stood
Between that vast sea and west wood!
How large and liberal her soul,
How confident, how purely chare,
How trusting; how untried the whole
Great heart, grand faith, that blossomed
there.

XVI.

Ay, she was as Madonna to
The tawny, lawless, faithful few
Who touched her hand and knew her soul:
She drew them, drew them as the pole
Points all things to itself.
She drew
Men upward as a moon of spring,

High wheeling, vast and bosom-full,
Half clad in clouds and white as wool,
Draws all the strong seas following.

Yet still she moved as sad, as lone
As that same moon that leans above,
And seems to search high heaven through
For some strong, all-sufficient love,
For one brave love to be her own,
To lean upon, to love, to woo,
To lord her high, white world, to yield
His clashing sword against her shield.

Oh, I once knew a sad, white dove
That died for such sufficient love,
Such high-born soul with wings to soar:
That stood up equal in its place,
That looked love level in the face,
Nor wearied love with leaning o'er
To lift love level where she trod
In sad delight the hills of God.

XVII.

How slow before the sleeping breeze,
That stranger ship from under seas !

How like to Dido by her sea,
When reaching arms imploringly,—
Her large, round, rich, impassioned arms,
Tossed forth from all her storied charms—
This one lone maiden leaning stood
Above that sea, beside the wood!
The ship crept strangely up the seas;

Her shrouds seemed shreds, her masts seemed
trees,—
Strange tattered trees of toughest bough
That knew no cease of storm till now.
The maiden pitied her; she prayed
Her crew might come, nor feel afraid;
She prayed the winds might come,—they
came,
As birds that answer to a name.

The maiden held her blowing hair
That bound her beauteous self about;
The sea-winds housed within her hair:
She let it go, it blew in rout
About her bosom full and bare.
Her round, full arms were free as air,
Her high hands clasped as clasped in prayer.

XVIII.

The breeze grew bold, the battered ship
Began to flap her weary wings;
The tall, torn masts began to dip
And walk the wave like living things.
She rounded in, she struck the stream,
She moved like some majestic dream.

The captain kept her deck. He stood
A Hercules among his men;
And now he watched the sea, and then
He peered as if to pierce the wood.
He now looked back, as if pursued,
Now swept the sea with glass as though
He fled or feared some hidden foe.

Swift sailing up the river's mouth,
Swift tacking north, swift tacking south,
He touched the overhanging wood;
He tacked his ship; his tall black mast
Touched tree-top mosses as he passed;
He touched the steep shore where she stood.

XIX.

Her hands still clasped as if in prayer,
Sweet prayer set to silentness;
Her sun-browned throat uplifted, bare
And beautiful.
Her eager face
Illumed with love and tenderness,
And all her presence gave such grace,
Dark shadowed in her cloud of hair,
That she seemed more than mortal fair.

XX.

He saw. He could not speak. No more
With lifted glass he sought the sea ;
No more he watched the wild new shore.
Now foes might come, now friends might flee;
He could not speak, he would not stir,—
He saw but her, he feared but her.

The black ship ground against the shore,
She ground against the bank as one

With long and weary journeys done,
That would not rise to journey more.

Yet still this Jason silent stood
And gazed against that sun-lit wood,
As one whose soul is anywhere.

All seemed so fair, so wondrous fair !
At last aroused, he stepped to land
Like some Columbus. They laid hand
On lands and fruits, and rested there.

XXI.

He found all fairer than fair morn
In sylvan land, where waters run
With downward leap against the sun,
And full-grown sudden May is born.
He found her taller than tall corn
Tiptoe in tassel ; found her sweet
As vale where bees of Hybla meet.

An unblown rose, an unread book ;
A wonder in her wondrous eyes ;

A large, religious, steadfast look
Of faith, of trust,—the look of one
New welcomed in her Paradise.

He read this book—read on and on
From titlepage to colophon :
As in cool woods, some summer day,
You find delight in some sweet lay,
And so entranced read on and on
From titlepage to colophon.

XXII.

And who was he that rested there,—
This Hercules, so huge, so rare,
This giant of a grander day,
This Theseus of a nobler Greece,
This Jason of the golden fleece?
And who was he? And who were they
That came to seek the hidden gold
Long hollowed from the pirate's hold?
I do not know. You need not care.

. . . . . .

They loved, this maiden and this man,

And that is all I surely know,—
The rest is as the winds that blow.
He bowed as brave men bow to fate,
Yet proud and resolute and bold;
She, coy at first, and mute and cold,
Held back and seemed to hesitate,—
Half frightened at this love that ran
Hard gallop till her hot heart beat
Like sounding of swift courser's feet.

XXIII.

Two strong streams of a land must run
Together surely as the sun
Succeeds the moon. Who shall gainsay
The fates that reign, that wisely reign?
Love is, love was, shall be again.
Like death, inevitable it is;
Perchance, like death, the dawn of bliss.
Let us, then, love the perfect day,
The twelve o'clock of life, and stop
The two hands pointing to the top,
And hold them tightly while we may.

XXIV.

How piteous strange is love! The walks
By wooded ways; the silent talks
Beneath the broad and fragrant bough.
The dark deep wood, the dense black dell,
Where scarce a single gold beam fell
From out the sun.
They rested now
On mossy trunk. They wandered then
Where never fell the feet of men.

Then longer walks, then deeper woods,
Then sweeter talks, sufficient sweet,
In denser, deeper solitudes,—
Dear careless ways for careless feet;
Sweet talks of paradise for two,
And only two to watch or woo.

She rarely spake. All seemed a dream
She would not waken from. She lay
All night but waiting for the day,
When she might see his face, and deem
This man, with all his perils passed,
Had found the Lotus-land at last.

XXV.

The year waxed fervid, and the sun
Fell central down. The forest lay
A-quiver in the heat. The sea
Below the steep bank seemed to run
A molten sea of gold.

Away
Against the gray and rock-built isles
That broke the molten watery miles
Where lonesome sea-cows called all day,
The sudden sun smote angrily.

Therefore the need of deeper deeps,
Of denser shade for man and maid,
Of higher heights, of cooler steeps,
Where all day long the sea-wind stayed.

They sought the rock-reared steep. The breeze
Swept twenty thousand miles of seas;
Had twenty thousand things to say,
Of love, of lovers of Cathay,
To lovers 'mid these high-held trees.

XXVI.

To left, to right, below the height,
Below the wood by wave and stream,
Plumed pampas grasses grew to gleam
And bend their lordly plumes, and run
And shake, as if in very fright
Before sharp lances of the sun.

They saw the tide-bound, battered ship
Creep close below against the bank;
They saw it cringe and shrink; it shrank
As shrinks some huge black beast with fear
When some uncommon dread is near.
They heard the melting resin drip,

As drip the last brave blood-drops when
Life's battle waxes hot with men.

XXVII.

Yet what to her were burning seas,
Or what to him was forest flame?
They loved; they loved the glorious trees,

The gleaming tides, or rise or fall;
They loved the lisping winds that came
From sea-lost spice-set isles unknown,
With breath not warmer than their own:
They loved, they loved,—and that was all.

XXVIII.

Full noon! Below the ancient moss
With mighty boughs high clanged across,
The man with sweet words, over-sweet,
Fell pleading, plaintive, at her feet.

He spake of love, of boundless love,—
Of love that knew no other land,
Or face, or place, or anything;
Of love that like the wearied dove
Could light nowhere, but kept the wing
Till she alone put forth her hand
And so received it in her ark
From seas that shake against the dark!

He clasped her hands, climbed past her knees,
Forgot her hands and kissed her hair,—

The while her two hands clasped in prayer,
And fair face lifted to the trees.

Her proud breast heaved, her pure proud
breast
Rose like the waves in their unrest
When counter storms possess the seas.
Her mouth, her arched, uplifted mouth,
Her ardent mouth that thirsted so,—
No glowing lovesong of the South
Can say; no man can say or know
The glory there, and so live on
Content without that glory gone!

Her face still lifted up. And she
Disdained the cup of passion he
Hard pressed her panting lips to touch.
She dashed it by despised, and she
Caught fast her breath. She trembled much,
And sudden rose full height, and stood
An empress in high womanhood:
She stood a tower, tall as when
Proud Roman mothers suckled men
Of old-time truth and taught them such.

XXIX.

Her soul surged vast as space is. She
Was trembling as a courser when
His thin flank quivers, and his feet
Touch velvet on the turf, and he
Is all afoam, alert and fleet
As sunlight glancing on the sea,
And full of triumph before men.

At last she bended some her face,
Half leaned, then put him back a pace,
And met his eyes.

Calm, silently
Her eyes looked deep into his eyes,—
As maidens down some mossy well
Do peer in hope by chance to tell
By image there what future lies
Before them, and what face shall be
The pole-star of their destiny.

Pure Nature's lover! Loving him
With love that made all pathways dim

And difficult where he was not,—
Then marvel not at form forgot.
And who shall chide? Doth priest know aught
Of sign, or holy unction brought
From over seas, that ever can
Make man love maid or maid love man
One whit the more, one bit the less,
For all his mummeries to bless?
Yea, all his blessings or his ban?

The winds breathed warm as Araby:
She leaned upon his breast, she lay
A wide-winged swan with folded wing.
He drowned his hot face in her hair,
He heard her great heart rise and sing;
He felt her bosom swell.
The air
Swooned sweet with perfume of her form.
Her breast was warm, her breath was warm,
And warm her warm and perfumed mouth
As summer journeys through the South.

XXX.

The argent sea surged steep below,

Surged languid in a tropic glow;
And two great hearts kept surging so!

The fervid kiss of heaven lay
Precipitate on wood and sea.
Two great souls glowed with ecstasy,
The sea glowed scarce as warm as they.

XXXI.

'Twas love's low amber afternoon.
Two far-off pheasants thrummed a tune,
A cricket clanged a restful air.
The dreamful billows beat a rune
Like heart regrets.

Around her head
There shone a halo. Men have said
'Twas from a dash of Titian
That flooded all her storm of hair
In gold and glory. But they knew,
Yea, all men know there ever grew
A halo round about her head
Like sunlight scarcely vanishèd.

XXXII.

How still she was! She only knew
His love. She saw no life beyond.
She loved with love that only lives
Outside itself and selfishness,—
A love that glows in its excess;
A love that melts pure gold, and gives
Thenceforth to all who come to woo
No coins but this face stamped thereon,—
Ay, this one image stamped upon
Its face, with some dim date long gone.

XXXIII.

They kept the headland high; the ship
Below began to chafe her chain,
To groan as some great beast in pain;
While white fear leapt from lip to lip:
"The woods are fire! the woods are flame!
Come down and save us in God's name!"

He heard! he did not speak or stir,—
He thought of her, of only her,

While flames behind, before them lay
To hold the stoutest heart at bay!

Strange sounds were heard far up the flood,
Strange, savage sounds that chilled the blood!
Then sudden from the dense, dark wood
Above, about them where they stood
A thousand beasts came peering out;
And now was thrust a long black snout,
And now a dusky mouth. It was
A sight to make the stoutest pause.

"Cut loose the ship!" the black mate cried;
"Cut loose the ship!" the crew replied.
They drove into the sea. It lay
As light as ever middle day.

The while their half-blind bitch that sat
All slobber-mouthed, and monkish cowled
With great, broad, floppy, leathern ears
Amid the men, rose up and howled,
And doleful howled her plaintive fears,
While all looked mute aghast thereat.
It was the grimmest eve, I think,
That ever hung on Hades' brink

Great broad-winged bats possessed the air,
Bats whirling blindly everywhere;
It was such troubled twilight eve
As never mortal would believe.

XXXIV.

Some say the crazed hag lit the wood
In circle where the lovers stood;
Some say the gray priest feared the crew
Might find at last the hoard of gold
Long hidden from the black ship's hold,—
I doubt me if men ever knew.
But such mad, howling, flame-lit shore
No mortal ever saw before.

Huge beasts above that shining sea,
Wild, hideous beasts with shaggy hair,
With red mouths lifting in the air,
They piteous howled, and plaintively,—
The wildest sounds, the weirdest sight
That ever shook the walls of night.

How lorn they howled, with lifted head,

To dim and distant isles that lay
Wedged tight along a line of red,
Caught in the closing gates of day
'Twixt sky and sea and far away,—
It was the saddest sound to hear
That ever struck on human ear.

They doleful called; and answered they
The plaintive sea-cows far away,—
The great sea-cows that called from isles,
Away across wide watery miles,
With dripping mouths and lolling tongue,
As if they called for captured young,—

The huge sea-cows that called the whiles
Their great wide mouths were mouthing moss;
And still they doleful called across
From isles beyond the watery miles.
No sound can half so doleful be
As sea-cows calling from the sea.

XXXV.

The drowned sun sank and died. He lay
In seas of blood. He sinking drew

The gates of sunset sudden to,
Where shattered day in fragments lay,
And night came, moving in mad flame;
The night came, lighted as he came,
As lighted by high summer sun
Descending through the burning blue.
It was a gold and amber hue,
And all hues blended into one.
The night spilled splendor where she came,
And filled the yellow world with flame.

The moon came on, came leaning low
Along the far sea-isles aglow;
She fell along that amber flood
A silver flame in seas of blood.
It was the strangest moon, ah me!
That ever settled on God's sea.

XXXVI.

Slim snakes slid down from fern and grass,
From wood, from fen, from anywhere;
You could not step, you would not pass,
And you would hesitate to stir,

Lest in some sudden, hurried tread
Your foot struck some unbruised head:

They slid in streams into the stream,—
It seemed like some infernal dream;
They curved, and graceful curved across,
Like graceful, waving sea-green moss,—
There is no art of man can make
A ripple like a rippling snake!

XXXVII.

Abandoned, lorn, the lovers stood,
Abandoned there, death in the air!
That beetling steep, that blazing wood—
Red flame! and red flame everywhere!
Yet was he born to strive, to bear
The front of battle. He would die
In noble effort, and defy
The grizzled visage of despair.

He threw his two strong arms full length
As if to surely test their strength;
Then tore his vestments, textile things
That could but tempt the demon wings

Of flame that girt them round about,
Then threw his garments to the air
As one that laughed at death, at doubt,
And like a god stood grand and bare.

She did not hesitate; she knew
The need of action; swift she threw
Her burning vestments by, and bound
Her wondrous wealth of hair that fell
An all-concealing cloud around
Her glorious presence, as he came
To seize and bear her through the flame,—
An Orpheus out of burning hell!

He leaned above her, wound his arm
About her splendor, while the noon
Of flood tide, manhood, flushed his face,
And high flames leapt the high headland!—
They stood as twin-hewn statues stand,
High lifted in some storied place.

He clasped her close, he spoke of death,—
Of death and love in the same breath.
He clasped her close; her bosom lay
Like ship safe anchored in some bay.

XXXVIII.

The flames! They could not stand or stay;
Before the beetling steep, the sea!
But at his feet a narrow way,
A short steep path, pitched suddenly
Safe open to the river's beach,
Where lay a small white isle in reach,—
A small, white, rippled isle of sand
Where yet the two might safely land.

And there, through smoke and flame, behold
The priest stood safe, yet all appalled!
He reached the cross; he cried, he called;
He waved his high-held cross of gold.
He called and called, he bade them fly
Through flames to him, nor bide and die!

Her lover saw; he saw, and knew
His giant strength would bear her through.
And yet he would not start or stir.
He clasped her close as death can hold,
Or dying miser clasp his gold,—
His hold became a part of her.

He would not give her up! He would
Not bear her waveward though he could!
That height was heaven; the wave was hell.
He clasped her close,—what else had done
The manliest man beneath the sun?
Was it not well? was it not well?

O man, be glad! be grandly glad,
And king-like walk thy ways of death!
For more than years of bliss you had
That one brief time you breathed her breath,
Yea, more than years upon a throne
That one brief time you held her fast,
Soul surged to soul, vehement, vast,—
True breast to breast, and all your own.

Live me one day, one narrow night,
One second of supreme delight
Like that, and I will blow like chaff
The hollow years aside, and laugh
A loud triumphant laugh, and I,
King-like and crowned, will gladly die.

Oh, but to wrap my love with flame!
With flame within, with flame without!

Oh, but to die like this, nor doubt—
To die and know her still the same!
To know that down the ghostly shore
Snow-white she waits me ever more!

XXXIX.

He poised her, held her high in air,—
His great strong limbs, his great arm's length!—
Then turned his knotted shoulders bare
As birth-time in his splendid strength,
And strode, strode with a lordly stride
To where the high and wood-hung edge
Looked down, far down upon the molten tide.
The flames leaped with him to the ledge,
The flames leapt leering at his side.

XL.

He leaned above the ledge. Below
He saw the black ship idly cruise,—
A midge below, a mile below.

His limbs were knotted as the thews
Of Hercules in his death-throe.

The flame! the flame! the envious flame!
She wound her arms, she wound her hair
About his tall form, grand and bare,
To stay the fierce flame where it came.

The black ship, like some moonlit wreck,
Below along the burning sea
Crept on and on all silently,
With silent pygmies on her deck.

That midge-like ship, far, far below;
That mirage lifting from the hill!
His flame-lit form began to grow,—
To grow and grow more grandly still.
The ship so small, that form so tall,
It grew to tower over all.

A tall Colossus, bronze and gold,
As if that flame-lit form were he
Who once bestrode the Rhodian sea,
And ruled the watery world of old:
As if the lost Colossus stood
Above that burning sea of wood.

And she that shapely form upheld,
Held high as if to touch the sky,
What airy shape, how shapely high,—
A goddess of the seas of eld!

Her hand upheld, her high right hand,
As if she would forget the land;
As if to gather stars, and heap
The stars like torches there to light
Her Hero's path across the deep
To some far isle that fearful night.

It was as if Colossus came,
Came proudly reaching from the flame
Above the sea in sheen of gold,
His sea-bride leaping from his hold;
The lost Colossus, and his bride
In bronze perfection at his side:
As if the lost Colossus came
Companioned from the past, his bride
With torch all faithful at his side:

With star-tipped torch that reached and
rolled
Through cloud-built corridors of gold:
His bride, austere and stern and grand,—

Bartholdi's goddess by the sea,
Far lifting, lighting Liberty
From prison seas to freedom's land.

XLI.

The flame! the envious flame, it leapt
Enraged to see such majesty,
Such scorn of death; such kingly scorn.
Then like some lightning-riven tree
They sank down in that flame—and slept
And all was hushed above that steep
So still that they might sleep and sleep;
As still as when a day is born.

At last! from out the embers leapt
Two shafts of light above the night,—
Two wings of flame that lifting swept
In steady, calm, and upward flight;
Two wings of flame against the white
Far-lifting, tranquil, snowy cone;
Two wings of love, two wings of light,

Far, far above that troubled night,
As mounting, mounting to God's throne.

XLII.

And all night long that upward light
Lit up the sea-cow's bed below:
The far sea-cows still calling so
It seemed as they must call all night.
All night! there was no night. Nay, nay,
There was no night. The night that lay
Between that awful eve and day,—
That nameless night was burned away.

THE RHYME OF THE GREAT RIVER.

PART I.

PART I.

RHYME on, rhyme on, in reedy flow,
O river, rhymer ever sweet!
The story of thy land is meet,
The stars stand listening to know.

Rhyme on, O river of the earth!
Gray father of the dreadful seas,
Rhyme on! the world upon its knees
Shall yet invoke thy wealth and worth.

Rhyme on, the reed is at thy mouth,
O kingly minstrel, mighty stream!
Thy Crescent City, like a dream,
Hangs in the heaven of my South.

Rhyme on, rhyme on! these broken strings
Sing sweetest in this warm south wind;
I sit thy willow banks and bind
A broken harp that fitful sings.

THE RHYME OF THE GREAT RIVER.

I.

AND where is my city, sweet blossom-sown
town?
And what is her glory, and what has she done?
By the Mexican seas in the path of the sun
Sit you down: in the crescent of seas sit you
down.

Ay, glory enough by my Mexican seas!
Ay, story enough in that battle-torn town,
Hidden down in the crescent of seas, hidden
down
'Mid mantle and sheen of magnolia-strewn trees.

But mine is the story of souls; of a soul
That bartered God's limitless kingdom for
gold,—
Sold stars and all space for a thing he could
hold
In his palm for a day, ere he hid with the mole.

O father of waters! O river so vast!
So deep, so strong, and so wondrous wild,—
He embraces the land as he rushes past,
Like a savage father embracing his child.

His sea-land is true and so valiantly true,
His leaf-land is fair and so marvelous fair,
His palm-land is filled with a perfumed air
Of magnolia blooms to its dome of blue.

His rose-land has arbors of moss-swept oak,—
Gray, Druid old oaks; and the moss that sways
And swings in the wind is the battle-smoke
Of duelists, dead in her storied days.

His love-land has churches and bells and chimes;
His love-land has altars and orange flowers;
And that is the reason for all these rhymes,—
These bells, they are ringing through all the hours!

His sun-land has churches and priests at prayer,
White nuns, as white as the far north snow;
They go where danger may bid them go,—
They dare when the angel of death is there.

His love-land has ladies so fair, so fair,
  In the Creole quarter, with great black eyes,
So fair that the Mayor must keep them there
  Lest troubles, like troubles of Troy, arise.

His love-land has ladies, with eyes held down,
  Held down, because if they lifted them,
Why, you would be lost in that old French town,
  Though you held even to God's garment hem.

His love-land has ladies so fair, so fair,
  That they bend their eyes to the holy book,
Lest you should forget yourself, your prayer,
  And never more cease to look and to look.

And these are the ladies that no men see,
  And this is the reason men see them not.
Better their modest sweet mystery,—
  Better by far than the battle-shot.

And so, in this curious old town of tiles.
  The proud French quarter of days long gone,
In castles of Spain and tumble-down piles
  These wonderful ladies live on and on.

I sit in the church where they come and go;
  I dream of glory that has long since gone,
Of the low raised high, of the high brought low,
  As in battle-torn days of Napoleon.

These piteous places, so rich, so poor!
  One quaint old church at the edge of the town
Has white tombs laid to the very church door,—
  White leaves in the story of life turned down.

White leaves in the story of life are these,
  The low white slabs in the long, strong grass,
  Where Glory has emptied her hour glass
And dreams with the dreamers beneath the trees.

I dream with the dreamers beneath the sod,
  Where souls pass by to the great white throne;
  I count each tomb as a mute milestone
For weary, sweet souls on their way to God.

I sit all day by the vast, strong stream,
  'Mid low white slabs in the long, strong grass
  Where time has forgotten for aye to pass,
To dream, and ever to dream and to dream.

This quaint old church with its dead to the door,
By the cypress swamp at the edge of the town,
So restful seems that you want to sit down
And rest you, and rest you for evermore.

And one white tomb is a lowliest tomb
That has crept up close to the crumbling door,—
Some penitent soul, as imploring room
Close under the cross that is leaning o'er.

'Tis a low white slab, and 't is nameless, too—
Her untold story, why, who should know?
Yet God, I reckon, can read right through
That nameless stone to the bosom below.

And the roses know, and they pity her, too;
They bend their heads in the sun or rain,
And they read, and they read, and then read again,
As children reading strange pictures through.

Why, surely her sleep it should be profound;
For, oh, the apples of gold above!

And, oh, the blossoms of bridal love!
And, oh, the roses that gather around!

The sleep of a night or a thousand morns?
Why, what is the difference here, to-day?
Sleeping and sleeping the years away
With all earth's roses and none of its thorns.

Magnolias white and the roses red—
The palm-tree here and the cypress there:
Sit down by the palm at the feet of the dead,
And hear a penitent's midnight prayer.

II.

The old churchyard is still as death,
A stranger passes to and fro
As if to church—he does not go—
The dead night does not draw a breath.

A lone sweet lady prays within.
The stranger passes by the door—
Will he not pray? Is he so poor
He has no prayer for his sin?

Is he so poor? His two strong hands
  Are full and heavy, as with gold;
They clasp, as clasp two iron bands
  About two bags with eager hold.

Will he not pause and enter in,
  Put down his heavy load and rest,
Put off his garmenting of sin,
  As some black burden from his breast?

Ah, me! the brave alone can pray.
  The church-door is as cannon's mouth
  To sinner North, or sinner South,
More dreaded than dread battle day.

Now two men pace. They pace apart,
  And one with youth and truth is fair;
The fervid sun is in his heart,
  The tawny South is in his hair.

Ay, two men pace, pace left and right—
  The lone, sweet lady prays within—
Ay, two men pace: the silent night
  Kneels down in prayer for some sin.

Lo! two men pace; and one is gray,
  A blue-eyed man from snow-clad land,
  With something heavy in each hand,—
With heavy feet, as feet of clay.

Ay, two men pace; and one is light
  Of step, but still his brow is dark;
  His eyes are as a kindled spark
That burns beneath the brow of night!

And still they pace. The stars are red,
  The tombs are white as frosted snow;
The silence is as if the dead
  Did pace in couples, to and fro.

III.

The azure curtain of God's house
  Draws back, and hangs star-pinned to
    space;
I hear the low, large moon arouse,
  I see her lift her languid face.

I see her shoulder up the east,
  Low-necked, and large as womanhood,—

Low-necked, as for some ample feast
  Of gods, within yon orange-wood.

She spreads white palms, she whispers peace,—
  Sweet peace on earth forevermore;
Sweet peace for two beneath the trees,
  Sweet peace for one within the door

The bent stream, like a scimitar
  Flashed in the sun, sweeps on and on,
  Till sheathed like some great sword new-drawn
In seas beneath the Carib's star.

The high moon climbs the sapphire hill,
  The lone, sweet lady prays within;
  The crickets keep a clang and din—
They are so loud, earth is so still!

And two men glare in silence there!
  The bitter, jealous hate of each
  Has grown too deep for deed or speech—
The lone sweet lady keeps her prayer.

The vast moon high through heaven's field
  In circling chariot is rolled;

The golden stars are spun and reeled,
  And woven into cloth of gold.

The white magnolia fills the night
  With perfume, as the proud moon fills
The glad earth with her ample light
  From out her awful sapphire hills.

White orange blossoms fill the boughs
  Above, about the old church door,—
They wait the bride, the bridal vows,—
  They never hung so fair before.

The two men glare as dark as sin!
  And yet all seems so fair, so white,
You would not reckon it was night,—
  The while the lady prays within.

IV.

She prays so very long and late,—
  The two men, weary, waiting there,—
The great magnolia at the gate
  Bends drowsily above her prayer.

The cypress in his cloak of moss,
  That watches on in silent gloom,
Has leaned and shaped a shadow-cross
  Above the nameless, lowly tomb.

What can she pray for? What her sin?
  What folly of a maid so fair?
  What shadows bind the wondrous hair
Of one who prays so long within?

The palm-trees guard in regiment,
  Stand right and left without the gate,
  The myrtle-moss trees wait and wait;
The tall magnolia leans intent.

The cypress trees, on gnarled old knees,
  Far out the dank and marshy deep
  Where slimy monsters groan and creep,
Kneel with her in their marshy seas.

What can her sin be? Who shall know?
  The night flies by,—a bird on wing;
The men no longer to and fro
  Stride up and down, or anything.

For one so weary and so old
  Has hardly strength to stride or stir;
He can but hold his bags of gold,—
  But hug his gold and wait for her.

The two stand still,—stand face to face.
  The moon slides on; the midnight air
  Is perfumed as a house of prayer—
The maiden keeps her holy place.

Two men! And one is gray, but one
  Scarce lifts a full-grown face as yet:
  With light foot on life's threshold set,—
Is he the other's sun-born son?

And one is of the land of snow,
  And one is of the land of sun;
  A black-eyed burning youth is one,
But one has pulses cold and slow:

Ay, cold and slow from clime of snow
  Where Nature's bosom, icy bound,
  Holds all her forces, hard, profound,—
Holds close where all the South lets go.

Blame not the sun, blame not the snows,
  God's great schoolhouse for all is clime,
  The great school-teacher, Father Time;
And each has borne as best he knows.

At last the elder speaks,—he cries,—
  He speaks as if his heart would break;
He speaks out as a man that dies,—
  As dying for some lost love's sake:

"Come, take this bag of gold, and go!
  Come, take one bag! See, I have two!
Oh, why stand silent, staring so,
  When I would share my gold with you?

"Come, take this gold! See how I pray!
  See how I bribe, and beg, and buy,—
Ay, buy! buy love, as you, too, may
  Some day before you come to die.

"God! take this gold, I beg, I pray!
  I beg as one who thirsting cries
  For but one drop of drink, and dies
In some lone, loveless desert way

"You hesitate? Still hesitate?
  Stand silent still and mock my pain?
Still mock to see me wait and wait,
  And wait her love, as earth waits rain?"

V.

O broken ship! O starless shore!
  O black and everlasting night,
Where love comes never any more
  To light man's way with heaven's light.

A godless man with bags of gold
  I think a most unholy sight;
  Ah, who so desolate at night
Amid death's sleepers still and cold?

A godless man on holy ground
  I think a most unholy sight.
I hear death trailing like a hound
  Hard after him, and swift to bite.

VI.

The vast moon settles to the west;
  Two men beside a nameless tomb,

And one would sit thereon to rest,—
  Ay, rest below, if there was room.

What is this rest of death, sweet friend?
  What is the rising up,—and where?
  I say, death is a lengthened prayer,
A longer night, a larger end

Hear you the lesson I once learned:
  I died; I sailed a million miles
  Through dreamful, flowery, restful isles,—
She was not there, and I returned.

I say the shores of death and sleep
  Are one; that when we, wearied, come
  To Lethe's waters, and lie dumb,
'Tis death, not sleep, holds us to keep.

Yea, we lie dead for need of rest,
  And so the soul drifts out and o'er
  The vast still waters to the shore
Beyond, in pleasant, tranquil quest:

It sails straight on, forgetting pain,
  Past isles of peace, to perfect rest,—

Now were it best abide, or best
Return and take up life again?

And that is all of death there is,
Believe me. If you find your love
In that far land, then like the dove
Abide, and turn not back to this.

But if you find your love not there;
Or if your feet feel sure, and you
Have still allotted work to do,—
Why, then return to toil and care.

Death is no mystery. 'Tis plain
If death be mystery, then sleep
Is mystery thrice strangely deep,—
For oh this coming back again!

Austerest ferryman of souls!
I see the gleam of solid shores,
I hear thy steady stroke of oars
Above the wildest wave that rolls.

O Charon, keep thy sombre ships!
We come, with neither myrrh nor balm,

Nor silver piece in open palm,
But lone white silence on our lips.

VII.

She prays so long! she prays so late!
What sin in all this flower-land
Against her supplicating hand
Could have in heaven any weight?

Prays she for her sweet self alone?
Prays she for some one far away,
Or some one near and dear to-day,
Or some poor, lorn, lost soul unknown?

It seems to me a selfish thing
To pray forever for one's self;
It seems to me like heaping pelf
In heaven by hard reckoning.

Why, I would rather stoop and bear
My load of sin, and bear it well
And bravely down to burning hell,
Than ever pray one selfish prayer!

VIII.

The swift chameleon in the gloom—
  This silence it is so profund!—
  Forsakes its bough, glides to the ground,
Then up, and lies across the tomb.

It erst was green as olive-leaf,
  It then grew gray as myrtle moss
  The time it slid the moss across;
But now 'tis marble-white with grief.

The little creature's hues are gone;
  Here in the pale and ghostly light
  It lies so pale, so panting white,—
White as the tomb it lies upon.

The two men by that nameless tomb.
  And both so still! You might have said
  These two men, they are also dead,
And only waiting here for room.

How still beneath the orange-bough!
  How tall was one, how bowed was one!

The one was as a journey done,
The other as beginning now.

And one was young,—young with that youth
Eternal that belongs to truth;
And one was old,—old with the years
That follow fast on doubts and fears.

And yet the habit of command
Was his, in every stubborn part;
No common knave was he at heart,
Nor his the common coward's hand.

He looked the young man in the face,
So full of hate, so frank of hate;
The other, standing in his place,
Stared back as straight and hard as fate.

And now he sudden turned away,
And now he paced the path, and now
Came back, beneath the orange-bough
Pale-browed, with lips as cold as clay.

As mute as shadows on a wall,
As silent still, as dark as they,

Before that stranger, bent and gray,
The youth stood scornful, proud, and tall.

He stood, a tall palmetto-tree
With Spanish daggers guarding it;
Nor deed, nor word, to him seemed fit
While she prayed on so silently.

He slew his rival with his eyes;
His eyes were daggers piercing deep,—
So deep that blood began to creep
From their deep wounds and drop wordwise:

His eyes so black, so bright that they
Might raise the dead, the living slay,
If but the dead, the living, bore
Such hearts as heroes had of yore:

Two deadly arrows barbed in black,
And feathered, too, with raven's wing;
Two arrows that could silent sting,
And with a death-wound answer back.

How fierce he was! how deadly still
In that mesmeric, hateful stare

Turned on the pleading stranger there
That drew to him, despite his will:

So like a bird down-fluttering,
Down, down, beneath a snake's bright eyes,
He stood, a fascinated thing,
That hopeless, unresisting, dies.

He raised a hard hand as before,
Reached out the gold, and offered it
With hand that shook as ague-fit,—
The while the youth but scorned the more.

"You will not touch it? In God's name
Who are you, and what are you, then?
Come, take this gold, and be of men,—
A human form with human aim.

"Yea, take this gold,—she must be mine
She shall be mine! I do not fear
Your scowl, your scorn, your soul austere,
The living, dead, or your dark sign.

"I saw her as she entered there;
I saw her, and uncovered stood:

The perfume of her womanhood
Was holy incense on the air.

"She left behind sweet sanctity,
Religion lay the way she went;
I cried I would repent, repent!
She passed on, all unheeding me.

"Her soul is young, her eyes are bright
And gladsome, as mine own are dim;
But, oh, I felt my senses swim
The time she passed me by to-night!—

"The time she passed, nor raised her eyes
To hear me cry I would repent,
Nor turned her head to hear my cries,
But swifter went the way she went,—

"Went swift as youth, for all these years!
And this the strangest thing appears,
That lady there seems just the same,—
Sweet Gladys—Ah! you know her name?

"You hear her name and start that I
Should name her dear name trembling so?

Why, boy, when I shall come to die
 That name shall be the last I know.

"That name shall be the last sweet name
 My lips shall utter in this life!
That name is brighter than bright flame,—
 That lady is my wedded wife!

"Ah, start and catch your burning breath!
 Ah, start and clutch your deadly knife!
If this be death, then be it death,—
 But that loved lady is my wife!

"Yea, you are stunned! your face is white,
 That I should come confronting you,
As comes a lorn ghost of the night
 From out the past, and to pursue.

"You thought me dead? You shake your head,
 You start back horrified to know
That she is loved, that she is wed,
 That you have sinned in loving so.

"Yet what seems strange, that lady there,
Housed in the holy house of prayer,

Seems just the same for all her tears,—
For all my absent twenty years.

"Yea, twenty years to night, to night,
Just twenty years this day, this hour,
Since first I plucked that perfect flower,
And not one witness of the rite.

"Nay, do not doubt,—I tell you true!
Her prayers, her tears, her constancy
Are all for me, are all for me,—
And not one single thought for you!

"I knew, I knew she would be here
This night of nights to pray for me!
And how could I for twenty year
Know this same night so certainly?

'Ah me! some thoughts that we would drown
Stick closer than a brother to
The conscience, and pursue, pursue
Like baying hound to hunt us down.

"And then, that date is history;
For on that night this shore was shelled,

And many a noble mansion felled,
With many a noble family.

"I wore the blue ; I watched the flight
Of shells, like stars tossed through the air,
To blow your hearth-stones—anywhere,
That wild, illuminated night.

"Nay, rage befits you not so well :
Why, you were but a babe at best,
Your cradle some sharp bursted shell
That tore, maybe, your mother's breast !

"Hear me ! We came in honored war.
The risen world was on your track !
The whole North-land was at our back,
From Hudson's bank to the North star !

"And from the North to palm-set sea.
The splendid fiery cyclone swept.
Your fathers fell, your mothers wept,
Their nude babes clinging to the knee.

"A wide and desolated track :
Behind, a path of ruin lay ;

Before, some women by the way
Stood mutely gazing, clad in black.

"From silent women waiting there
Some tears came down like still, small rain ;
Their own sons on the battle plain
Were now but viewless ghosts of air.

"Their own dear daring boys in gray,—
They should not see them any more ;
Our cruel drums kept telling o'er
The time their own sons went away.

"Through burning town, by bursting shell—
Yea, I remember well that night ;
I led through orange-lanes of light,
As through some hot outpost of hell !

"That night of rainbow shot and shell
Sent from your surging river's breast
To waken me, no more to rest,—
That night I should remember well !

"That night amid the maimed and dead,—
A night in history set down

By light of many a burning town,
And written all across in red,—

"Her father dead, her brothers dead,
Her home in flames,—what else could she
But fly all helpless here to me,
A fluttered dove, that night of dread?

"Short time, hot time had I to woo
Amid the red shells' battle-chime;
But women rarely reckon time,
And perils speed their love when true.

"And then I wore a captain's sword;
And, too, had oftentime before
Doffed cap at her dead father's door,
And passed a soldier's pleasant word.

"And then—ah, I was comely then!
I bore no load upon my back,
I heard no hounds upon my track,
But stood the tallest of tall men.

"Her father's and her mother's shrine,
This church amid the orange wood,

So near and so secure it stood,
It seemed to beckon as a sign.

"Its white cross seemed to beckon me:
My heart was strong, and it was mine
To throw myself upon my knee,
To beg to lead her to this shrine.

"She did consent. Through lanes of light
I led through that church-door that night—
Let fall your hand! Take back your face
And stand,—stand patient in your place!

"She loved me; and she loves me still.
Yea, she clung close to me that hour
As honey-bee to honey-flower,—
And still is mine, through good or ill.

"The priest stood there. He spake the prayer;
He made the holy, mystic sign.
And she was mine, was wholly mine,—
Is mine this moment I will swear!

"Then days, then nights, of vast delight,—
Then came a doubtful, later day;

The faithful priest, now far away,
Watched with the dying in the fight:

"The priest amid the dying, dead,
Kept duty on the battle-field,—
That midnight marriage unrevealed
Kept strange thoughts running through my head.

"At last a stray ball struck the priest:
This vestibule his chancel was;
And now none lived to speak her cause,
Record, or champion her the least.

"Hear me! I had been bred to hate
All priests, their mummeries and all.
Ah, it was fate,—ah, it was fate
That all things tempted me to fall!

"And then the rattling songs we sang
Those nights when rudely revelling,—
The songs that only soldiers sing,—
Until the very tent-poles rang!

"What is the rhyme that rhymers say
Of maidens born to be betrayed

By epaulettes and shining blade,
While soldiers love and ride away?

"And then my comrades spake her name
Half taunting, with a touch of shame;
Taught me to hold that lily-flower
As some light pastime of the hour.

"And then the ruin in the land,
  The death, dismay, the lawlessness!
Men gathered gold on every hand,—
  Heaped gold: and why should I do less?

"The cry for gold was in the air,
  For Creole gold, for precious things;
The sword kept prodding here and there
  Through bolts and sacred fastenings.

"'Get gold! get gold!' This was the cry.
And I loved gold. What else could I
Or you, or any earnest one
Born in this getting age have done?

"With this one lesson taught from youth,
  And ever taught us, to get gold,—

To get and hold, and ever hold,—
What else could I have done, forsooth?

"She, seeing how I sought for gold,—
This girl, my wife, one late night told
Of treasures hidden close at hand,
In her dead father's mellow land;

"Of gold she helped her brothers hide
Beneath a broad banana tree
The day the two in battle died,
The night she dying fled to me.

"It seemed too good; I laughed to scorn
Her trustful tale. She answered not;
But meekly on the morrow morn
Two massive bags of bright gold brought.

"And when she brought this gold to me,
Red Creole gold, rich, rare, and old,—
When I at last had gold, sweet gold,
I cried in very ecstacy.

"Red gold! rich gold! two bags of gold!
The two stout bags of gold she brought

And gave with scarce a second thought,—
Why, her two hands could scarcely hold!

"Now I had gold! two bags of gold!
Two wings of gold, to fly, and fly
The wide world's girth; red gold to hold
Against my heart for aye and aye!

"My country's lesson: 'Gold! get gold!'
I learned it well in land of snow;
And what can glow, so brightly glow
Long winter nights of northern cold?

"Ay, now at last, at last I had
The one thing, all fair things above
My land had taught me most to love!
A miser now! and I grew mad.

"With these two bags of gold my own,
I then began to plan that night
For flight, for far and sudden flight,—
For flight; and, too, for flight alone.

"I feared! I feared! My heart grew cold,—
Some one might claim this gold of me!

I feared her,—feared her purity—
Feared all things but my bags of gold.

"I grew to hate her face, her creed,—
That face the fairest ever yet
That bowed o'er holy cross or bead,
Or yet was in God's image set.

"I fled,—nay, not so knavish low
As you have fancied, did I fly;
I sought her at that shrine, and I
Told her full frankly I should go.

"I stood a giant in my power,—
And did she question or dispute?
I stood a savage, selfish brute,—
She bowed her head, a lily-flower.

"And when I sudden turned to go,
And told her I should come no more,
She bowed her head so low, so low,
Her vast black hair fell pouring o'er.

"And that was all; her splendid face
Was mantled from me, and her night

Of hair half hid her from my sight
  As she fell moaning in her place.

"And there, 'mid her dark night of hair,
  She sobbed, low moaning through her tears,
  That she would wait, wait all the years,—
Would wait and pray in her despair.

"Nay, did not murmur, not deny,—
  She did not cross me one sweet word!
  I turned and fled: I thought I heard
A night-bird's piercing low death-cry!"

THE RHYME OF THE GREAT RIVER.

PART II.

HOW soft the moonlight of the South!
How sweet my South in soft moonlight!
I want to kiss her warm sweet mouth
As she lies sleeping here to-night.

How still! I do not hear a mouse.
I see some bursting buds appear;
I hear God in His garden,—hear
Him trim some flowers for His house.

I hear some singing stars; the mouth
Of my vast river sings and sings,
And pipes on reeds of pleasant things,—
Of splendid promise for my South:

My great South-woman, soon to rise
And tiptoe up and loose her hair;
Tiptoe, and take from all the skies
God's stars and glorious moon to wear!

I.

THE poet shall create or kill,
 Bid heroes live, bid braggarts die.
I look against a lurid sky,—
 My silent South lies proudly still.

The lurid light of burning lands
 Still climbs to God's house overhead;
Mute women wring white withered hands;
 Their eyes are red, their skies are red.

Poor man! still boast your bitter wars!
 Still burn and burn, and burning die.
But God's white finger spins the stars
 In calm dominion of the sky.

And not one ray of light the less
 Comes down to bid the grasses spring;
 No drop of dew nor anything
Shall fail for all your bitterness.

The land that nursed a nation's youth,
 Ye burned it, sacked it, sapped it dry.

Ye gave it falsehoods for its truth,
  And fame was fashioned from a lie.

If man grows large, is God the less?
  The moon shall rise and set the same,
  The great sun spill his splendid flame
And clothe the world in queenliness.

And from that very soil ye trod
  Some large-souled seeing youth shall come
  Some day, and he shall not be dumb
Before the awful court of God.

II.

The weary moon had turned away,
  The far North-Star was turning pale
  To hear the stranger's boastful tale
Of blood and flame that battle day.

And yet again the two men glared,
  Close face to face above that tomb;
  Each seemed as jealous of the room
The other eager waiting shared.

Again the man began to say,—
As taking up some broken thread,
As talking to the patient dead,—
The Creole was as still as they:

"That night we burned yon grass-grown town,—
The grasses, vines are reaching up;
The ruins they are reaching down,
As sun-browned soldiers when they sup.

"I knew her,—knew her constancy.
She said, this night of every year
She here would come, and kneeling here,
Would pray the live-long night for me.

"This praying seems a splendid thing!
It drives old Time the other way;
It makes him lose all reckoning
Of years that pagans have to pay.

"This praying seems a splendid thing!
It makes me stronger as she prays—
But oh the bitter, bitter days
When I became a banished thing!

"I fled, took ship,—I fled as far
As far ships drive tow'rd the North Star:
For I did hate the South, the sun
That made me think what I had done.

"I could not see a fair palm tree
In foreign land, in pleasant place,
But it would whisper of her face
And shake its keen, sharp blades at me.

"Each black-eyed woman would recall
A lone church-door, a face, a name,
A coward's flight, a soldier's shame:
I fled from woman's face, from all.

"I hugged my gold, my precious gold,
Within my strong, stout, buckskin vest.
I wore my bags against my breast
So close I felt my heart grow cold.

"I did not like to see it now;
I did not spend one single piece,
I travelled, travelled without cease
As far as Russian ship could plow.

"And when my own scant hoard was gone,
And I had reached the far North-land,
I took my two stout bags in hand
As one pursued, and journeyed on.

"Ah, I was weary! I grew gray;
I felt the fast years slip and reel
As slip black beads when maidens kneel
At altars when out-door is gay.

"At last I fell prone in the road,—
Fell fainting with my cursed load.
A skin-clad cossack helped me bear
My bags, nor would one shilling share.

"He looked at me with proud disdain,—
He looked at me as if he knew;
His black eyes burned me thro' and thro';
His scorn pierced like a deadly pain.

"He frightened me with honesty;
He made me feel so small, so base,
I fled, as if the fiend kept chase,—
The fiend that claims my company!

"I bore my load alone; I crept
Far up the steep and icy way;
And there, before a cross there lay
A barefoot priest, who bowed and wept.

"I threw my gold right down and sped
Straight on. And, oh, my heart was light!
A spring-time bird in spring-time flight
Flies not so happy as I fled.

"I felt somehow this monk would take
My gold, my load from off my back;
Would turn the fiend from off my track,
Would take my gold for sweet Christ's sake!

"I fled; I did not look behind;
I fled, fled with the mountain wind.
At last, far down the mountain's base
I found a pleasant resting-place.

"I rested there so long, so well,
More grateful than all tongues can tell.
It was such pleasant thing to hear
That valley's voices calm and clear.

"That valley veiled in mountain air,
With white goats on the hills at morn;
That valley green with seas of corn,
With cottage islands here and there.

"I watched the mountain girls. The hay
They mowed was not more sweet than they;
They laid brown hands in my white hair;
They marveled at my face of care.

"I tried to laugh; I could but weep.
I made these peasants one request,—
That I with them might toil or rest,
And with them sleep the long, last sleep.

"I begged that I might battle there,
For that fair valley-land, for those
Who gave me cheer when girt with foes,
And have a country, loved and fair.

"Where is that spot that poets name
Our country? name the hallowed land?
Where is that spot where man must stand
Or fall when girt with sword and flame?

"Where is that one permitted spot?
Where is the one place man must fight?
Where rests the one God-given right
To fight, as ever patriots fought?

"I say 't is in that holy house
Where God first set us down on earth:
Where mother welcomed us at birth,
And bared her breasts, a happy spouse.

"But when some wrong, some deed of shame,
Shall make that land no more our own—
Ah! hunger for that holy name
My country, I have truly known!

"The simple plough-boy from his field
Looks forth. He sees God's purple wall
Encircling him. High over all
The vast sun wheels his shining shield.

"This King, who makes earth what it is,—
King David bending to his toil!
O lord and master of the soil,
How envied in thy loyal bliss!

"Long live the land we loved in youth,—
That world with blue skies bent about,
Where never entered ugly doubt!
Long live the simple, homely truth!

"Can true hearts love some far snow-land,
Some bleak Alaska bought with gold?
God's laws are old as love is old;
And Home is something near at hand.

"Yea, change yon river's course; estrange
The seven sweet stars; make hate divide
The full moon from the flowing tide,—
But this old truth ye can not change.

"I begged a land as begging bread;
I begged of these brave mountaineers
To share their sorrows, share their tears;
To weep as they wept, with their dead.

"They did consent. The mountain town
Was mine to love, and valley lands.
That night the barefoot monk came down
And laid my two bags in my hands!

"On! on! And, oh, the load I bore!
Why, once I dreamed my soul was lead;
Dreamed once it was a body dead!
It made my cold, hard bosom sore.

"I dragged that body forth and back—
O conscience, what a baying hound!
Nor frozen seas nor frosted ground
Can throw this bloodhound from his track.

"In farthest Russia I lay down
A dying man, at last to rest;
I felt such load upon my breast
As seamen feel, who sinking drown.

"That night, all chill and desperate,
I sprang up, for I could not rest;
I tore the two bags from my breast,
And dashed them in the burning grate.

"I then crept back into my bed;
I tried, I begged, I prayed to sleep;
But those red, restless coins would keep
Slow dropping, dropping, and blood red.

"I heard them clink and clink and clink,—
They turned, they talked within that grate.
They talked of her, they made me think
Of one who still must pray and wait.

"And when the bags burned crisp and black,
Two coins did start, roll to the floor,—
Roll out, roll on, and then roll back,
As if they needs must journey more.

"Ah, then I knew nor change nor space,
Nor all the drowning years that rolled
Could hide from me her haunting face,
Nor still that red-tongued talking gold.

"Again I sprang forth from my bed!
I shook as in an ague fit;
I clutched that red gold, burning red,
I clutched as if to strangle it.

"I clutched it up—you hear me, boy?—
I clutched it up with joyful tears!
I clutched it close, with such wild joy
I had not felt for years and years!

"Such joy! for I should now retrace
My steps, should see my land, her face;
Bring back her gold this battle day,
And see her, see her, hear her pray!

"I brought it back—you hear me, boy?—
I clutch it, hold it, hold it now:
Red gold, bright gold that giveth joy
To all, and anywhere or how;

"That giveth joy to all but me,—
To all but me, yet soon to all.
It burns my hands, it burns! but she
Shall ope my hands and let it fall.

"For oh I have a willing hand
To give these bags of gold; to see
Her smile as once she smiled on me
Here in this pleasant warm palm-land."

He ceased, he thrust each hard-clenched fist,
He threw his gold hard forth again,
As one impelled by some mad pain
He would not or could not resist.

The creole, scorning, turned away,
  As if he turned from that lost thief,—
  The one that died without belief
That awful crucifixion day.

III.

Believe in man, nor turn away.
  Lo! man advances year by year;
  Time bears him upward, and his sphere
Of life must broaden day by day.

Believe in man with large belief;
  The garnered grain each harvest-time
  Hath promise, roundness, and full prime
For all the empty chaff and sheaf.

Believe in man with proud belief:
  Truth keeps the bottom of her well,
And when the thief peeps down, the thief
  Peeps back at him, perpetual.

Faint not that this or that man fell;
  For one that falls a thousand rise

To lift white Progress to the skies:
  Truth keeps the bottom of her well.

Fear not for man, nor cease to delve
  For cool, sweet truth, with large belief
Lo! Christ himself chose only twelve,
  Yet one of these turned out a thief

IV.

Down through the dark magnolia leaves
  Where climbs the rose of Cherokee
  Against the orange-blossomed tree,
A loom of moonlight weaves and weaves,—

A loom of moonlight, weaving clothes
  From snow-white rose of Cherokee,
  And bridal blooms of orange-tree,
For fairy folk in fragrant rose.

Down through the mournful myrtle crape,
  Through moving moss, through ghostly
    gloom,
A long white moonbeam takes a shape
  Above a nameless, lowly tomb;

A long white finger through the gloom
  Of grasses gathered round about,—
  As God's white finger pointed out
A name upon that nameless tomb.

V.

Her white face bowed in her black hair,
  The maiden prays so still within
  That you might hear a falling pin,—
Ay, hear her white unuttered prayer

The moon has grown disconsolate,
  Has turned her down her walk of stars:
  Why, she is shutting up her bars,
As maidens shut a lover's gate.

The moon has grown disconsolate;
She will no longer watch and wait.
But two men wait; and two men will
Wait on till morning, mute and still:

Still wait and walk among the trees,
  Quite careless if the moon may keep

Her walk along her starry steep
Above the Southern pearl-sown seas.

They know no moon, or set or rise
Of stars, or anything to light
The earth or skies, save her dark eyes,
This praying, waking, watching night.

They move among the tombs apart,
Their eyes turn ever to that door;
They know the worn walks there by heart—
They turn and walk them o'er and o'er:

They are not wide, these little walks
For dead folk by this crescent town;
They lie right close when they lie down,
As if they kept up quiet talks.

VI.

The two men keep their paths apart;
But more and more begins to stoop
The man with gold, as droop and droop
Tall plants with something at their heart.

Now once again with eager zest
  He offers gold with silent speech;
  The other will not walk in reach,
But walks around, as round a pest.

His dark eyes sweep the scene around,
  His young face drinks the fragrant air,
  His dark eyes journey everywhere,—
The other's cleave unto the ground.

It is a weary walk for him,
  For oh he bears a weary load!
  He does not like that narrow road
Between the dead—it is so dim:

It is so dark, that narrow place,
  Where graves lie thick, like yellow leaves:
Give us the light of Christ and grace,
  Give light to garner in the sheaves.

Give light of love; for gold is cold,
  And gold is cruel as a crime;
  It gives no light at such sad time
As when man's feet wax weak and old.

Ay, gold is heavy, hard, and cold!
  And have I said this thing before?
  Well, I will tell it o'er and o'er,
'Twere need be told ten thousand fold.

"Give us this day our daily bread,"—
  Get this of God, then all the rest
  Is housed in thine own honest breast,
If you but lift a lordly head.

VII.

Oh, I have seen men, tall and fair,
  Stoop down their manhood with disgust,
  Stoop down God's image to the dust,
To get a load of gold to bear;

Have seen men selling day by day
  The glance of manhood that God gave:
  To sell God's image as a slave
Might sell some little pot of clay!

Behold! here in this green graveyard
  A man with gold enough to fill

A coffin, as a miller's till;
And yet his path is hard, so hard!

His feet keep sinking the sand,
And now so near an opened grave!
He seems to hear the solemn wave
Of dread oblivion at hand.

The sands, they grumble so, it seems
As if he walks some shelving brink,
He tries to stop, he tries to think,
He tries to make believe he dreams:

Why, he is free to leave the land,
The silver moon is white as dawn;
Why, he has gold in either hand,
Has silver ways to walk upon.

And who should chide, or bid him stay?
Or taunt, or threat, or bid him fly?
The world's for sale I hear men say,
And yet this man has gold to buy.

Buy what? Buy rest? He could not rest!
Buy gentle sleep? He could not sleep,

Though all these graves were wide and deep
  As their wide mouths with the request.

Buy Love, buy faith, buy snow-white truth?
  Buy moonlight, sunlight, present, past?
Buy but one brimful cup of youth
  That calm souls drink of to the last?

O God! 't is pitiful to see
  This miser so forlorn and old!
O God! how poor a man may be
  With nothing in this world but gold!

VIII.

The broad magnolia's blooms are white;
  Her blooms are large, as if the moon
Had lost her way some lazy night,
  And lodged here till the afternoon.

Oh, vast white blossoms breathing love!
  White bosom of my lady dead,
  In your white heaven overhead
I look, and learn to look above.

IX.

All night the tall magnolia kept
  Kind watch above the nameless tomb:
  Two shapes kept waiting in the gloom
And gray of morn, where roses wept.

The dew-wet roses wept; their eyes
  All dew, their breath as sweet as prayer.
  And as they wept the dead down there
Did feel their tears and hear their sighs.

The grass uprose as if afraid
  Some stranger foot might press too near;
  Its every blade was like a spear
Its every spear a living blade.

The grass above that nameless tomb
  Stood all arrayed, as if afraid
Some weary pilgrim seeking room
  And rest, might lay where she was laid.

X.

'T was morn, and yet it was not morn;
  'T was morn in heaven, not on earth,—

A star was singing of a birth,
Just saying that a day was born.

The marsh hard by that bound the lake,—
The great low sea-lake, Ponchartrain,
Shut off from sultry Cuban main,—
Drew up its legs, as half awake.

Drew long stork legs, long legs that steep
In slime where aligators creep,—
Drew long green legs that stir the grass,
As when the late lorn night-winds pass.

Then from the marsh came croakings low,
Then louder croaked some sea-marsh beast;
Then, far away against the east,
God's rose of morn began to grow.

From out the marsh, against that east,
A ghostly moss-swept cypress stood;
With ragged arms above the wood
It rose, a God-forsaken beats.

It seemed so frightened where it rose!
The moss-hung thing it seemed to wave

The worn-out garments of the grave,—
To wave and wave its old grave-clothes.

Close by, a cow rose up and lowed
From out a palm-thatched milking-shed.
A black boy on the river road
Fled sudden, as the night had fled:

A nude black boy, a bit of night
That had been broken off and lost
From flying night, the time it crossed
The surging river in its flight:

A bit of darkness, following
The sable night on sable wing,—
A bit of darkness stilled with fear,
Because that nameless tomb was near.

Then holy bells came pealing out;
Then steamboats blew, then horses neighed;
Then smoke from hamlets round about
Crept out, as if no more afraid.

Then shrill cocks here, and shrill cocks there,
Stretched glossy necks and filled the air.

How many cocks it takes to make
A country morning well awake!

Then many boughs, with many birds,—
  Young boughs in green, old boughs in gray,
  These birds had very much to say
In their soft, sweet, familiar words.

And all seemed sudden glad; the gloom
Forgot the church, forgot the tomb;
And yet like monks with cross and bead
The myrtles leaned to read and read.

And oh the fragrance of the sod!
  And oh the perfume of the air!
  The sweetness, sweetness everywhere,
That rose like incense up to God!

I like a cow's breath in sweet spring,
  I like the breath of babes new-born;
A maid's breath is a pleasant thing,—
  But oh the breath of sudden morn!

Of sudden morn, when every pore
  Of mother earth is pulsing fast

With life, and life seems spilling o'er
  With love, with love too sweet to last:

Of sudden morn beneath the sun,
  By God's great river wrapped in gray,
That for a space forgets to run,
  And hides his face as if to pray.

XI.

The black-eyed Creole kept his eyes
  Turned to the door, as eyes might turn
  To see the holy embers burn
Some sin away at sacrifice.

Full dawn! but yet he knew no dawn,
  Nor song of bird, nor bird on wing,
  Nor breath of rose, nor anything
Her fair face lifted not upon.

And yet he taller stood with morn;
  His bright eyes, brighter than before,
  Burned fast against that fastened door,
His proud lips lifting up with scorn,—

With lofty, silent scorn for one
  Who all night long had plead and plead,
  With none to witness but the dead
How he for gold must be undone.

Oh, ye who feed a greed for gold,
  And barter truth, and trade sweet youth
For cold hard gold, behold, behold!
  Behold this man! behold this truth!

Why, what is there in all God's plan
  Of vast creation, high or low,
  By sea or land, by sun or snow,
So mean, so miserly as man?

Lo, earth and heaven all let go
  Their garnered riches, year by year!
The treasures of the trackless snow,
  Ah, hast thou seen how very dear?

The wide earth gives, gives golden grain,
  Gives fruits of gold, gives all, gives all!
  Hold forth your hand, and these shall fall
In your full palm as free as rain.

Yea, earth is generous. The trees
  Strip nude as birth-time without fear,
  And their reward is year by year
To feel their fulness but increase.

The law of Nature is to give,
  To give, to give! and to rejoice
  In giving with a generous voice,
And so trust God and truly live.

But see this miser at the last,—
  This man who loves, grasps hold of gold,
  Who grasps it with such eager hold,
To hold forever hard and fast:

As if to hold what God lets go;
  As if to hold, while all around
  Lets go, and drops upon the ground
All things as generous as snow.

Let go your greedy hold, I say!
  Let go your hold! Do not refuse
  'Till death comes by and shakes you loose,
And sends you shamed upon your way.

What if the sun should keep his gold ?
  The rich moon lock her silver up ?
  What if the gold-clad buttercup
Became a miser, mean and old ?

Ah, me ! the coffins are so true
  In all accounts, the shrouds so thin,
That down there you might sew and sew,
  Nor ever sew one pocket in.

And all that you can hold of lands
  Down there, below the grass, down there,
  Will only be that little share
You hold in your two dust-full hands.

XII.

She comes! she comes! The stony floor
Speaks out! And now the rusty door
At last has just one word this day,
With mute religious lips, to say.

She comes! she comes! And lo, her face
  Is upward, radiant, fair as prayer!

So pure here in this holy place,
  Where holy peace is everywhere.

Her upraised face, her face of light
  And loveliness, from duty done,
  Is like a rising orient sun
That pushes back the brow of night.

How brave, how beautiful is truth!
  Good deeds untold are like to this.
  But fairest of all fair things is
A pious maiden in her youth:

A pious maiden as she stands
  Just on the threshold of the years
  That throb and pulse with hopes and fears,
And reaches God her helpless hands.

How fair is she! How fond is she!
  Her foot upon the threshold there.
Her breath is as a blossomed tree,—
  This maiden mantled in her hair!

Her hair, her black, abundant hair,
  Where night, inhabited all night

And all this day, will not take flight,
But finds content and houses there.

Her hands are clasped, her two small hands:
They hold the holy book of prayer
Just as she steps the threshold there,
Clasped downward where she silent stands.

XIII.

Once more she lifts her lowly face,
And slowly lifts her large, dark eyes
Of wonder, and in still surprise
She looks full forward in her place.

She looks full forward on the air
Above the tomb, and yet below
The fruits of gold, the blooms of snow,
As looking—looking anywhere.

She feels—she knows not what she feels;
It is not terror, is not fear,
But there is something that reveals
A presence that is near and dear.

She does not let her eyes fall down,
  They lift against the far profound:
Against the blue above the town
  Two wide-winged vultures circle round.

Two brown birds swim above the sea,—
Her large eyes swim as dreamily
And follow far, and follow high,
Two circling black specks in the sky.

One forward step,—the closing door
  Creaks out, as frightened or in pain;
  Her eyes are on the ground again—
Two men are standing close before.

"My love," sighs one, "my life, my all!"
  Her lifted foot across the sill
  Sinks down,—and all things are so still
You hear the orange blossoms fall.

But fear comes not where duty is,
  And purity is peace and rest;
  Her cross is close upon her breast,
Her two hands clasp hard hold of this.

Her two hands clasp cross, book, and she
Is strong in tranquil purity,—
Ay, strong as Samson when he laid
His two hands forth, and bowed and prayed.

One at her left, one at her right,
  And she between, the steps upon,—
I can but see that Syrian night,
  The women there at early dawn.

'T is strange, I know, and may be wrong,
But, ever, pictured in my song;
And rhyming on, I see the day
They came to roll the stone away.

XIV.

The sky is like an opal sea,
  The air is like the breath of kine,
But, oh, her face is white and she
  Leans faint to see a lifted sign,—

To see two hands lift up and wave
  To see a face so white with woe,

So ghastly, hollow, white as though
It had that moment left the grave.

Her sweet face at that ghostly sign,
Her fair face in her weight of hair,
Is like a white dove drowning there,—
A white dove drowned in Tuscan wine.

He tries to stand, to stand erect,
'Tis gold, 'tis gold that holds him down!
And soul and body both must drown,—
Two millstones tied about his neck.

Now once again his piteous face
Is raised to her face reaching there.
He prays, such piteous, silent prayer,
As prays a dying man for grace.

It is not good to see him strain
To lift his hands, to gasp, to try
To speak. His parched lips are so dry
Their sight is as a living pain.

I think that rich man down in hell
Some like this old man with his gold,—

To gasp and gasp perpetual
  Like to this minute I have told.

XV.

At last the miser cries his pain,—
  A shrill, wild cry, as if a grave
  Just ope'd its stony lips and gave
One sentence forth, then closed again.

" 'Twas twenty years last night, last night!"
  His lips still moved, but not to speak;
His outstretched hands so trembling weak
  Were beggar's hands in sorry plight.

His face upturned to hers, his lips
  Kept talking on, but gave no sound;
  His feet were cloven to the ground;
Like iron hooks his finger tips.

" Ay, twenty years," she sadly sighed:
  "I promised mother every year,
  That I would pray for father here,
As she had prayed, the night she died:

"To pray as she prayed, fervidly;
 As she had promised she would pray
 The sad night of her marriage day,
For him, wherever he might be."

Then she was still; then sudden she
 Let fall her eyes, and so outspake
 As if her very heart would break,
Her proud lips trembling piteously:

"And whether he comes soon or late
 To kneel beside this nameless grave,
May God forgive my father's hate
 As I forgive, as she forgave!"

He saw the stone; he understood,
 With that quick knowledge that will come
 Most quick when men are made most dumb
With terror that stops still the blood.

And then a blindness slowly fell
 On soul and body; but his hands
 Held tight his bags, two iron bands,
As if to bear them into hell.

He sank upon the nameless stone
With, oh, such sad, such piteous moan
As never man might seek to know
From man's most unforgiving foe.

He sighed at last, so long, so deep,
As one's heart breaking in one's sleep,—
One long, last, weary, willing sigh,
As if it were a grace to die.

And then his hands, like loosened bands,
  Hung down, hung down on either side;
  His hands hung down and opened wide:
He rested in the orange lands.

ISLES OF THE AMAZONS.

PART I.

PRIMEVAL forests! virgin sod!
That Saxon has not ravish'd yet
Lo! peak on peak in stairways set--
In stepping stairs that reach to God!
Here we are free as sea or wind,
For here are set Time's snowy tents
In everlasting battlements
Against the march of Saxon mind.

FAR up in the hush of the Amazon River,
And mantled and hung in the tropical trees,
There are isles as grand as the isles of the seas
And the waves strike strophes, and keen reeds quiver,
As the sudden canoe shoots a-past them and over
The strong, still tide to the opposite shore,
Where the blue-eyed men by the sycamore
Sit mending their nets 'neath the vine-twined cover;

Sit weaving their threads of bark and grasses,
They wind and they spin, on the clumsy wheel,
Into hammocks red-hued with the cochineal,
To trade with the single black ship that passes,
With foreign old freightage of curious old store,
And as still and as slow as if half asleep,—
A cunning old trader that loves to creep
Above and a-down in the shade of the shore.

And the blue-eyed men that are mild as the dawns—
Oh, delicate dawns of the grand Andes!—
Lift up soft eyes that are deep like seas,
And mild yet wild as the red-white fawns';

And they gaze into yours, then weave, then listen,
Then look in wonder, then again weave on,
Then again look wonder that you are not gone,
While the keen reeds quiver and the bent waves glisten;

But they say no words while they weave and wonder,

Though they sometimes sing, voiced low like
the dove,
And as deep and as rich as their tropical love,
A-weaving their net threads through and under.

Yea, a pure, true people you may trust are
these,
That weave their threads where the quick
leaves quiver;
And this is their tale of the Isles of the river,
And the why that their eyes are so blue like
seas,
And the why that the men draw water and bear
The wine or the water in the wild boar skin,
And do live in the woods and do weave and
spin,
And so bear with the women full burthen and
share.

A curious old tale of a curious old time,
That is told you betimes by a quaint old crone,
Who sits on the rim of an island alone,
As ever was told you in story or rhyme.

Her brown, bare feet dip down to the river,
And dabble and plash to her monotone tone,

As she holds in her hands a strange green
stone,
And talks to the boat where the bent reeds
quiver.

And the quaint old crone has a singular way
Of holding her head to the side and askew,
And smoothing the stone in her palms all day
As saying "I've nothing at all for you,"
Until you have anointed her palm, and you
Have touched on the delicate spring of a
door
That silver has opened perhaps before;
For woman is woman the wide world through.

The old near truth on the far new shore
I bought and I paid for it; so did you:
The tale may be false or the tale may be true;
I give it as I got it, and who can more?

If I have made journeys to difficult shores,
And woven delusions in innocent verse,
If none be the wiser, why, who is the worse?
The field it was mine, the fruit it is yours.

A sudden told tale. You may read as you run.
A part of it hers, some part is my own,
Crude, and too carelessly woven and sown,
As I sail'd on the Mexican seas in the sun.

'Twas nations ago, when the Amazons were,
That a fair young knight—says the quaint old crone,
With her head sidewise, as she smoothes at the stone—
Came over the seas, with his golden hair,
And a great black steed, and glittering spurs,
And a sword that had come from crusaders down,
And a womanly face in a manly frown,
And a heart as tender and as true as hers.

And fairest, and foremost in love as in war
Was the brave young knight of the brave old days.
Of all the knights, with their knightly ways,
That had journey'd away to the world afar
In the name of Spain; of the splendid few
Who bore her banner in the new-born world,

From the sea rim up to where clouds are
curl'd,
And the condors beat their wings in the blue.

He was born, says the crone, where the brave
are fair,
And blown from the banks of the Guadal-
quiver,
And yet blue-eyed, with the Celt's soft hair,
With never a drop of the dark, deep river
Of Moorish blood that had swept through Spain,
And plash'd the world with its tawny stain.

His heart it rebell'd and arose with pity;
He sat on his steed, and his sword was bloody
With heathen blood: the battle was done;
And crown'd in fire, wreathed and ruddy
With antique temples built up to the sun,
Below on the plain lay the beautiful city
At the conqueror's feet; the red street strewn
With dead, with gold, and with gods over-
thrown.

He raised his head with a proud disdain,
He rein'd his steed on the reeking plain,
As the heathen pour'd, in a helpless flood,

With never a wail and with never a blow,
At last, to even provoke a foe,
Through gateways, wet with the pagan's blood.

"Ho, forward! smite!" but the minstrel linger'd,
He reach'd his hand and he touch'd the rein,
He humm'd an air, and he toy'd and finger'd
The arching neck and the glossy mane.

He rested the heel, he rested the hand,
Though the thing was death to the man to dare
To doubt, to question, to falter there,
Nor heeded at all to the hot command.

He wiped his steel on his black steed's mane,
He sheathed it deep, then look'd at the sun,
Then counted his comrades, one by one,
With booty return'd from the plunder'd plain.

He lifted his face to the flashing snow,
He lifted his shield of steel as he sang,
And he flung it away till it clang'd and rang
On the granite rocks in the plain below,

Then cross'd his bosom. Made overbold,

He lifted his voice and sang, quite low
At first, then loud in the long ago,
When a love endured though the days grew old.

They heard his song, the chief on the plain
Stood up in his stirrups, and, sword in hand,
He cried and he call'd with a loud command
To the blue-eyed boy to return again;
To lift his shield again to the sky,
And come and surrender his sword or die.

He wove his hand in the stormy mane,
He lean'd him forward, he lifted the rein,
He struck the flank, he wheel'd and sprang,
And gaily rode in the face of the sun,
And bared his sword and he bravely sang,
"Ho! come and take it!" but there came not one.

And so he sang with his face to the south:
"I shall go; I shall search for the Amazon shore,
Where the curses of man they are heard no more,
And kisses alone shall embrace the mouth.

"I shall journey in search of the Incan Isles,
  Go far and away to traditional land,
Where Love is a queen in a crown of smiles,
  And battle has never imbrued a hand;

"Where man has never despoil'd or trod,
  Where woman's hand with a woman's heart
  Has fashion'd an Eden from man apart,
And she walks in her garden alone with God.

"I shall seek that Eden, and all my years
  Shall sit and repose, shall sing in the sun;
  And the tides may rest or the tides may run,
And men may water the world with tears:

"And the years may come and the years may go,
  And men make war, may slay and be slain,
But I not care, for I never shall know
  Of man, or of aught that is man's again.

"The waves may battle, the winds may blow,
  The mellow rich moons may ripen and fall,
  The seasons of gold they may gather or go,
The mono may chatter, the paroquet call,
And who shall take heed, take note, or shall
      know

If the Fates befriend, or if ill befall,
Of worlds without, or of worlds at all,
Of heaven above, or of hades below."

'Twas the song of a dream and the dream of a singer,
Drawn fine as the delicate fibres of gold,
And broken in two by the touch of a finger,
And blown as the winds blow, rent and roll'd
In dust, and spent as a tale that is told.

Alas! for his dreams and the songs he sung;
The beasts beset him; the serpents they hung,
Red-tongued and terrible, over his head.
He clove and he thrust with his keen, quick steel,
He coax'd with his hand, he urged with his heel,
Till his steel was broken, and his steed lay dead.

He toil'd to the river, he lean'd intent
To the wave, and away through the fringe of boughs,
From beasts that pursued; and breathed his vows,
For soul and body were well-nigh spent.

'Twas the king of rivers, and the Isles were near;
Yet it moved so strange, so still, so strong,
It gave no sound, not even the song
Of a sea-bird screaming defiance or fear.

It was dark and dreadful! Wide like an ocean,
Much like a river but more like a sea,
Save that there was naught of the turbulent motion
Of tides, or of winds blown back, or a-lee.

Yea, strangely strong was the wave and slow,
And half-way hid in the dark deep tide,
Great turtles they paddled them to and fro,
And away to the Isles and the opposite side.

The nude black boar through abundant grass
Stole down to the water and buried his nose,
And crunch'd white teeth till the bubbles rose
As white and as bright as are globes of glass.

Yea, steadily moved it, mile upon mile,
Above and below and as still as the air;
The bank made slippery here and there
By the slushing slide of the crocodile.

The great trees bent to the tide like slaves;
They dipp'd their boughs as the stream swept on,
And then drew back, then dipp'd and were gone,
Away to the seas with the resolute waves.

The land was the tide's; the shore was undone;
It look'd as the lawless, unsatisfied seas
Had thrust up an arm through the tangle of trees,
And clutch'd at the citrons that grew in the sun;

And clutch'd at the diamonds that hid in the sand,
And laid heavy hand on the gold, and a hand
On the redolent fruits, on the ruby-like wine,
And the stones like the stars when the stars are divine;
Had thrust through the rocks of the ribb'd Andes;
Had wrested and fled; and had left a waste
And a wide way strewn in precipitate haste,
As he bore them away to the buccaneer seas.

O, heavens, the eloquent song of the silence!
Asleep lay the sun in the vines, on the sod,

And asleep in the sun lay the green-girdled islands,
As rock'd to their rest in the cradle of God.

God's poet is silence! His song is unspoken,
And yet so profound, so loud, and so far,
It fills you, it thrills you with measures unbroken,
And as still, and as fair, and as far as a star.

The shallow seas moan. From the first they have mutter'd,
As a child that is fretted, and wept at their will. . .
The poems of God are too grand to be utter'd:
The dreadful deep seas they are loudest when still.

"I shall fold my hands, for this is the river
Of death," he said, "and the sea-green isle
Is an Eden set by the gracious Giver
Wherein to rest." He listen'd the while,
Then lifted his head, then lifted a hand
Arch'd over his brow, and he lean'd and listen'd,—

'Twas only a bird on a border of sand,—
The dark stream eddied and gleam'd and glisten'd,
Stately and still as the march of a moon,
And the martial notes from the isle were gone,—
Gone as a dream dies out with the dawn,
And gone as far as the night from the noon.

'Twas only a bird on a border of sand,
Slow piping, and diving it here and there,
Slim, grey, and shadowy, light as the air,
That dipp'd below from a point of the land.

"Unto God a prayer and to love a tear,
And I die," he said, "in a desert here,
So deep that never a note is heard
But the listless song of that soulless bird."

The strong trees lean'd in their love unto trees.
Lock'd arms in their loves, and were so made strong,
Stronger than armies; aye, stronger than seas
That rush from their caves in a storm of song,

"A miser of old, his last great treasure
  Flung far in the sea, and he fell and he died;
  And so shall I give, O terrible tide,
To you my song and my last sad measure."

He blew on a reed by the still, strong river,
  Blew low at first, like a dream, then long,
Then loud, then loud as the keys that quiver,
  And fret and toss with their freight of song.

He sang and he sang with a resolute will,
  Till the mono rested above on his haunches,
And held his head to the side and was still,—
  Till a bird blown out of the night of branches,
  Sang sadder than love, so sweeter than sad,
Till the boughs did burthen and the reeds did fill
  With beautiful birds, and the boy was glad.

Our loves they are told by the myriad-eyed stars,
  Yet love it is well in a reasonable way,
  And fame it is fair in its way for a day,
Borne dusty from books and bloody from wars;
And death, I say, is an absolute need,
  And a calm delight, and an ultimate good;
But a song that is blown from a watery reed

By a soundless deep from a boundless wood,
With never a hearer to heed or to prize
But God and the birds and the hairy wild beasts,
Is sweeter than love, than fame, or than feasts,
Or any thing else that is under the skies.

The quick leaves quiver'd, and the sunlight danced;
As the boy sang sweet, and the birds said, "Sweet;"
And the tiger crept close, and lay low at his feet,
And he sheathed his claws as he gazed entranced.

The serpent that hung from the sycamore bough,
And sway'd his head in a crescent above,
Had folded his neck to the white limb now,
And fondled it close like a great black love.

But the hands grew weary, the heart wax'd faint,
The loud notes fell to a far-off plaint,
The sweet birds echo'd no more, "Oh, sweet,"
The tiger arose and unsheathed his claws,
The serpent extended his iron jaws,

And the frail reed shiver'd and fell at his feet.
A sound on the tide, and he turn'd and cried,
"Oh, give God thanks, for they come they come!"
He look'd out afar on the opaline tide,
Then clasp'd his hands, and his lips were dumb.

A sweeping swift crescent of sudden canoes!
As light as the sun of the south and as soon,
And true and as still as a sweet half-moon
That leans from the heavens, and loves and woos!

The Amazons came in their martial pride,
As full on the stream as a studding of stars,
All girded in armor as girded in wars,
In foamy white furrows dividing the tide.

With a face as brown as the boatmen's are,
Or the brave, brown hand of a harvester;
The Queen on a prow stood splendid and tall,
As petulant waters would lift and fall;
Stood forth for the song, half lean'd in surprise,
Stood fair to behold, and yet grand to behold,

And austere in her face, and saturnine-soul'd,
And sad and subdued, in her eloquent eyes.

And sad were they all; yet tall and serene
Of presence, but silent, and brow'd severe
As for some things lost, or for some fair, green,
And beautiful place, to the memory dear.

"O Mother of God! Thrice merciful saint!
I am saved!" he said, and he wept outright;
Ay, wept as even a woman might,
For the soul was full and the heart was faint.

"Stay! stay!" cried the Queen, and she leapt to
the land,
And she lifted her hand, and she lowered
their spears,
"A woman! a woman! ho! help! give a hand!
A woman! a woman! we know by the tears."

Then gently as touch of the truest of woman,
They lifted him up from the earth as he fell,
And into the boat, with a half hidden swell
Of the heart that was holy and tenderly hu-
man.

They spoke low-voiced as a vesper prayer;
They pillow'd his head as only the hand
Of woman can pillow, and push'd from the land,
And the Queen she sat threading the gold of his hair.

Then away with the wave, and away to the Isles,
In a song of the oars of the crescented fleet
That timed together in musical wiles
And bubbles of melodies swift and sweet.

PART II.

FORSAKE the People. What are they
That laugh, that live, that love by rule?
Forsake the Saxon. What are these
That shun the shadows of the trees.
The Druid forests? . . . Go thy way,
We are not one. I will not please
You:—fare you well, O wiser fool!

But you who love me;—Ye who love
The shaggy forests, fierce delights
Of sounding waterfalls, of heights
That hang like broken moons above,
With brows of pine that brush the sun,
Believe and follow. We are one;
The wild man shall to us be tame;
The woods shall yield their mysteries;
The stars shall answer to a name,
And be as birds above the trees.

THEY swept to the Isles through the furrows of foam,
They alit on the land as love hastening home,
And below the banana, with leaf like a tent,
They tenderly laid him, they bade him take rest,
They brought him strange fishes and fruits of the best,
And he ate and took rest with a patient content.

They watch'd him well; he rose up strong;
He stood in their midst, and they said, "How fair!"
And they said, "How tall!" And they toy'd with his hair.
And they touched his limbs and they said, "How long!
And how strong they are; and how brave she is,.
That she made her way through the wiles of man,
That she braved his wrath that she broke the ban
Of his desolate life for the love of this!"

They wrought for him armor of cunning attire,
They brought him a sword and a great shell shield,
And implored him to shiver the lance on the field,
And to follow their beautiful Queen in her ire.

But he took him apart; then the Amazons came
And entreated of him with their eloquent eyes
And their earnest and passionate souls of flame,

And the soft, sweet words that are broken of
 sighs,
To be one of their own; but he still denied
And bow'd and abash'd he stole further aside.

He stood by the Palms and he lean'd in unrest,
 And standing alone, looked out and afar,
 For his own fair land where the castles are,
With irresolute arms on a restless breast.
He re-lived his loves, he recall'd his wars,
 He gazed and he gazed with a soul distress'd,
 Like a far sweet star that is lost in the west,
Till the day was broken to a dust of stars.

They sigh'd, and they left him alone in the care
 Of faithfullest matron; they moved to the field
 With the lifted sword and the sounding shield
High fretting magnificent storms of hair.
And, true as the moon in her march of stars,
 The Queen stood forth in her fierce attire
Worn as they trained or worn in the wars,
 As bright and as chaste as a flash of fire.

With girdles of gold and of silver cross'd,
 And plaited, and chased, and bound together,

Broader and stronger than belts of leather,
Cunningly fashion'd and blazon'd and boss'd—
With diamonds circling her, stone upon stone,
Above the breast where the borders fail,
Below the breast where the fringes zone,
She moved in a glittering garment of mail.

The form made hardy and the waist made spare
From athlete sports and adventures bold,
The breastplate, fasten'd with clasps of gold,
Was clasp'd, as close as the breasts could bear,—
And bound and drawn to a delicate span,
It flash'd in the red front ranks of the field—
Was fashion'd full trim in its intricate plan
And gleam'd as a sign, as well as a shield,
That the virgin Queen was unyielding still,
And pure as the tides that around her ran;
True to her trust, and strong in her will
Of war, and hatred to the touch of man.

The field it was theirs in storm or in shine,
So fairly they stood that the foe came not
To the battle again, and the fair forgot
The rage of battle; and they trimm'd the vine,
They tended the fields of the tall green corn,

They crush'd the grape and they drew the wine
In great round gourds or the bended horn,
And seemed as souls that are half divine.

They bathed in the wave in the amber morn,
They took repose in the peaceful shade
Of eternal palms, and were never afraid;
Yet oft did they sigh, and look far and forlorn.

Where the rim of the wave was weaving a spell,
And the grass grew soft where it hid from the
sun,
Would the Amazons gather them every one
At the call of the Queen or the sound of her shell:

Would come in strides through the kingly trees,
And train and marshal them brave and well
In the golden noon, in the hush of peace
Where the shifting shades of the fan palms
fell;
Would train till flush'd and as warm as wine,
Would reach with their limbs, would thrust
with the lance,
Attack, retire, retreat and advance,
Then wheel in column, then fall in line;

Stand thigh and thigh with the limbs made hard
And rich and round as the swift limb'd pard,
Or a racer train'd, or a white bull caught
In the lasso's toils, where the tame are not:

Would curve as the waves curve, swerve in line;
Would dash through the trees, would train with the bow,
Then back to the lines, now sudden, then slow,
Then flash their swords in the sun at a sign;
Would settle the foot right firm afront,
Then sound the shield till the sound was heard
Afar, as the horn in the black boar hunt;
Yet, strangest of all, say never one word.

When shadows fell far from the westward, and when
The sun had kiss'd hands and made sail for the east,
They would kindle the fires and gather them then,
Well-worn and most merry with song, to the feast.
They sang of all things, but the one, sacred one,

That could make them most glad, as they lifted the gourd
And pass'd it around, with its rich purple hoard,
From the Island that lay with its front to the sun.

Though lips were most luscious, and eyes as divine
As the eyes of the skies that bend down from above;
Though hearts were made glad and most mellow with love,
As dripping gourds drain'd of their burthens of wine;
Though brimming, and dripping, and bent of their shape
Were the generous gourds from the juice of the grape,
They could sing not of love, they could breathe not a thought
Of the savor of life; of love sought, or unsought.

Their loves they were not; they had banish'd the name

Of man, and the uttermost mention of love,—
The moonbeams about them, the quick stars above,
The mellow-voiced waves, they were ever the same,
In sign, and in saying, of the old true lies;
But they took no heed; no answering sign,
Save glances averted and half-hush'd sighs,
Went back from the breasts with their loves divine.

They sang of their freedom with a will, and well,
They paid for it well when the price was blood;
They beat on the shield, and they blew on the shell,
When their wars were not, for they held it good
To be glad and to sing till the flush of the day,
In an annual feast, when the broad leaves fell;
Yet some sang not, and some sighed "Ah, well!"—
For there's far less left you to sing or to say,
When mettlesome love is banish'd, I ween,—
To hint at as hidden, or to half disclose
In the swift sword-cuts of the tongue, made keen
With wine at a feast,—than one would suppose.

So the days wore by, but they brought no rest
To the minstrel knight, though the sun was as gold,
And the Isles were green, and the great Queen blest
In the splendor of arms, and as pure as bold.

He would now resolve to reveal to her all,
His sex and his race in a well-timed song;
And his love of peace, his hatred of wrong,
And his own deceit, though the sun should fall.
Then again he would linger, and knew not how
He could best proceed, and deferr'd him now
Till a favorite day, then the fair day came,
And still he delay'd, and reproachd him the same.

And he still said nought, but, subduing his head,
He wander'd by day in a dubious spell
Of unutterable thought of the truth unsaid,
To the indolent shore, and he gather'd a shell,
And he shaped its point to his passionate mouth,
And he turn'd to a bank and began to blow,
While the Amazons trained in a troop below,
And as soft and as sweet as a kiss of the south.

The Amazons lifted with glad surprise,
  Stood splendid at first and look'd far and fair,
  Set forward a foot, and shook back their hair,
Like clouds push'd back from the sun-lit skies.

It stirr'd their souls, and they ceased to train
In troop by the shore, as the tremulous strain
Fell down from the hill through the tasselling
    trees;
And a murmur of song, like the sound of bees
In the clover crown of a queenly spring,
  Came back unto him, and he laid the shell
Aside on the bank, and began to sing
  Of eloquent love; and the ancient spell
Of passionate song was his, and the Isle,
  As waked to delight from its slumber long,
Came back in echoes; yet all this while
  He knew not at all the sin of his song.

PART III.

I KNOW upon this earth a spot
Where clinking coins, that clank as chains
Upon the souls of men, are not;
Nor man is measured for his gains
Of gold that streams with crimon stains.

The snow-topp'd towers crush the clouds
And break the still abode of stars,
Like sudden ghosts in snowy shrouds,
New broken through their earthly bars,
And condors whet their crooked beaks
On lofty limits of the peaks.

O men that fret as frets the main!
You irk me with your eager gaze
Down in the earth for fat increase—
Eternal talks of gold and gain,
Your shallow wit, your shallow ways,
And breaks my soul across the shoal
As breakers break on shallow seas.

THEY bared their brows to the palms above,
But some look'd level into comrades' eyes,
And they then remember'd that the thought of love
Was the thing forbidden, and they sank in sighs.

They turned from the training, to heed in throng
To the old, old tale; and they trained no more,
As he sang of love; and some on the shore,
And full in the sound of the eloquent song,
With a womanly air and irresolute will
Went listlessly onward as gathering shells;
Then gazed in the waters, as bound in spells;
Then turned to the song and so sigh'd, and were still.

And they said no word. Some tapp'd on the sand
With the sandal'd foot, keeping time to the sound,
In a sort of dream; some timed with the hand,
And one held eyes full of tears to the ground.
She thought of the days when their wars they were not,
As she lean'd and listened to the old, old song,
When they sang of their loves, and she well forgot
The hard oppressions and a world of wrong.

Like a pure true woman, with her trust in tears
And the things that are true, she re-lived them in thought,
Though hush'd and crush'd in the fall of the years;
She lived but the fair, and the false she forgot
As a tale long told, or as things that are dreams;
And the quivering curve of the lip it confest
The silent regrets, and a soul that teems
With a world of love in a brave true breast.

Then this one, younger, who had known no love,
Nor look'd upon man but in blood on the field,
She bow'd her head, and she leaned on her shield,
And her heart beat quick as the wings of a dove
That is blown from the sea, where the rests are not
In the time of storms; and by instinct taught
Grew pensive, and sigh'd; as she thought and she thought
Of some wonderful things, and—she knew not of what.

Then this one thought of a love forsaken,

She thought of a brown sweet babe, and she thought
Of the bread-fruits gather'd, of the swift fish taken
In intricate nets, like a love well sought.
She thought of the moons of her maiden dawn,
Mellow'd and fair with the forms of man;
So dearer indeed to dwell upon
Than the beautiful waves that around her ran;
So fairer indeed than the fringes of light
That lie at rest on the west of the sea
In furrows of foam on the borders of night,
And dearer indeed than the songs to be—
Than calling of dreams from the opposite land,
To the land of life, and of journeys dreary,
When the soul goes over from the form grown weary,
And walks in the cool of the trees on the strand.

But the Queen was enraged and would smite him at first
With the sword unto death, yet it seemed that she durst
Not touch him at all; and she moved as to chide,
And she lifted her face, and she frown'd at his side,

Then touch'd on his arm; then she looked in
his eyes
And right full in his soul, but she saw no fear,
In the pale fair face, and with frown severe
She press'd her lips as suppressing her sighs.

She banish'd her wrath, she unbended her face,
She lifted her hand and put back his hair
From his fair sad brow, with a penitent air,
And forgave him all with an unuttered grace.
But she said no word, yet no more was severe;
She stood as subdued by the side of him still,
Then averted her face with a resolute will,
As to hush a regret, or to hide back a tear.

She sighed to herself; "A stranger is this,
And ill and alone, that knows not at all
That a throne shall totter and the strong shall
fall,
At the mention of love and its banefullest bliss,
O life that is lost in bewildering love—
But a stranger is sacred!" She lifted a hand
And she laid it as soft as the breast of a dove
On the minstrel's mouth. It was more than
the wand

Of the tamer of serpents, for she did no more
Than to bid with her eyes and to beck with her hand,
And the song drew away to the waves of the shore;
Took wings, as it were, to the verge of the land.

But her heart was oppress'd. With penitent head
She turn'd to her troop, and, retiring, she said:
"Alas! and alas! shall it come to pass
That the panther shall die from a blade of grass?
That the tiger shall yield at the bent-horn blast?
That we, who have conquer'd a world and all
Of men and of beasts in the world must fall
Ourselves at the mention of love, at last?"

The singer was fretted, and farther apart
He wander'd, perplex'd; and he felt his heart
Beat quick and troubled, and all untamed,
As he saw her move with marvelous grace
To her troop below; he turn'd from his place,
Oppress'd and humbled, and sore ashamed
That he lived in the land in the shield of a lie;

That he dared not stand forth face to face
To the truth, and die as a knight should die.

The tall Queen turn'd to her troop,
She led the minstrel and all to the innermost
part
Of the palm-crown'd Isle, where great trees
group
In armies, to battle when black storms start,
And made her retreat from the sun by the trees
That are topp'd like tents, where the fire-flies
Are a light to the feet, and a fair lake lies
As cool as the coral-set centres of seas.

The palm-trees lorded the copse like kings,
Their tall tops tossing the indolent clouds
That folded the Isle in the dawn, like shrouds,
Then fled from the sun like to living things.
The cockatoo swung in the vines below,
And muttering hung on a golden thread,
Or moved on the moss'd bough to and fro,
In plumes of gold and array'd in red.

The lake lay hidden away from the light,
As asleep in the Isle from the tropical noon,

And narrow and bent like a new-born moon,
And fair as a moon in the noon of the night.
'Twas shadow'd by forests, and fringed by ferns,
And fretted anon by the fishes that leapt
At indolent flies that slept or kept
Their drowsy tones on the tide by turns.

And here in the dawn when the day was strong
And newly aroused from leafy repose,
With dews on his feet and tints of the rose
In his great flush'd face was a sense and song
That the tame old world has nor known nor heard.
The soul was fill'd with the soft perfumes,
The eloquent wings of the humming bird
Beguiled the heart, they purpled the air
And allured the eye, as so everywhere
On the rim of the wave or across it in rings,
They swept or they sank in a sea of blooms,
And wove and wound in a song of rings.

A bird in scarlet and gold, made mad
With sweet delights, through the branches slid
And kiss'd the lake on a drowsy lid
Till the ripples ran and the face was glad:

Was glad and lovely as lights that sweep
The face of heaven when the stars are forth
In autumn time through the awful north,
Or the face of a child when it smiles in sleep.

And here was the Queen, in the tropical noon,
When the wave and the world and all were asleep,
And nothing look'd forth to betray or to peep
Through glories of jungle in garments of June,
To bathe with her court in the waters that bent
In the beautiful lake through tasseling trees,
And the tangle of blooms in a burden of bees,
As bold and as sharp as a bow unspent.

And strangely still, and more strangely sweet,
Was the lake that lay in its cradle of fern,
As still as a moon with her horns that turn
In the night, like lamps to some delicate feet.

They came and they stood by the brink of the tide,
They hung their shields on the boughs of the trees,
They lean'd their lances against the side,

Unloosed their sandals, and busy as bees
Ungather'd their robes in the rustle of leaves
That wound them as close as the wine-vine
weaves.

The minstrel here falter'd, and further aside
Than ever before he averted his head;
He pick'd up a pebble and fretted the tide,
Then turn'd with a countenance flush'd and
red,

He feign'd him ill, he wander'd away,
He sat him down by the waters alone,
And pray'd for pardon, as a knight should pray,
And rued an error not all his own.

The Amazons press'd to the girdle of reeds,
Two and by two they advanced to the wave,
They challenged each other, and bade be
brave,
And banter'd, and vaunted of valorous deeds.
They push'd and they parted the curtains of
green,
All timid at first; then looked at the wave
And laugh'd; retreated, then came up brave
To the brink of the water, led on by their Queen.

Again they retreated, again advanced,
And parted the boughs in a proud disdain,
Then bent their heads to the waters, and glanced
Below, then blush'd, and then laugh'd again,
A bird awaken'd; then all dismayed
With a womanly sense of a beautiful shame
That strife and changes had left the same,
They shrank to the leaves and the sombre shade.

At last, press'd forward a beautiful pair
And bent to the wave, and bending they blush'd
As rich as their wines; when the waters rush'd
To the dimpled limbs, and laugh'd in their hair.

The fair troop follow'd with shouts and cheers,
They cleft the wave, and the friendly ferns
Came down in curtains and curves and turns,
And a brave palm lifted a thousand spears.

From under the ferns and away from the land,
And out in the wave until lost below,
There lay, as white as a bank of snow,
A long and a beautiful border of sand.

Here clothed alone in their clouds of hair
  And curtain'd about by the palm and fern,
And made as their maker had made them, fair,
  And splendid of natural curve and turn;
Untramell'd by art and untroubled by man
  They tested their strength, or tried their speed.
And here they wrestled, and there they ran,
  As supple and lithe as the watery reed.

The great trees shadow'd the bow-tipp'd tide,
And nodded their plumes from the opposite side,
  As if to whisper, Take care! take care!
  But the meddlesome sunshine here and there
Kept pointing a finger right under the trees,—
  Kept shifting the branches and wagging a hand
  At the round brown limbs on the border of sand,
And seem'd to whisper, Ho! what are these?

The gold-barr'd butterflies to and fro
  And over the waterside wander'd and wove
  As heedless and idle as clouds that rove
And drift by the peaks of perpetual snow.

A monkey swung out from a bough in the skies,

White-whisker'd and ancient, and wisest of all
Of his populous race, and he heard them call
And he watch'd them long, with his head side-
wise,
From under his brows of amber and brown,
All patient and silent, and never once stirr'd;
Then he shook his head, and he hasten'd him
down
To his army below and said never a word.

PART IV.

THERE is many a love in the land, my love,
But never a love like this is;
Then kill me dead with your love, my love,
And cover me up with kisses.

Yea, kill me dead and cover me deep
Where never a soul discovers;
Deep in your heart to sleep to sleep
In the darlingest tomb of lovers.

THE wanderer took him apart from the place;
Look'd up in the boughs at the gold birds there,
He counted the humming-birds fretting the air,
And brush'd at the butterflies fanning his face.

He sat him down in a crook of the wave
And away from the Amazons, under the skies
Where great trees curved to a leaf-lined cave,
And he lifted his hands and he shaded his eyes;

And he held his head to the north when they
came
To run on the reaches of sand from the south,
And he pull'd at his chin, and he pursed his
mouth,
And he shut his eyes, with a sense of shame.

He reach'd and he shaped him, sad and slow,
A bambo reed from the brink below;
He lifted it then and began to blow
As if to himself; as the sea sometimes
Does soothe and soothe in a low, sweet song,
When his rage is spent, and the beach swells
strong
With sweet repetitions of alliterate rhymes.

The echoes blew black from the indolent land;
Silent and still sat the tropical bird,
And only the sound of the reed was heard,
As the Amazons ceased from their sports on
the sand.

They rose from the wave, and inclining the
head,
They listen'd intent, with the delicate tip

Of the finger touch'd to the pouting lip,
Till the brown Queen turn'd in the tide, and led
Through the opaline lake, and under the shade,
To the shore where the chivalrous singer played.

He bended his head and he shaded his eyes
As well as he might with his lifted fingers,
And ceased to sing. But in mute surprise
He saw them linger as a child that lingers
Allured by a song thrown down through the street,
And looks bewilder'd about from its play,
For the last loved notes that fall at its feet;
And as he heard them whisper, he felt them sway
Aside and before all silent and sweet.

But the singer was vexed; he averted his head;
He lifted his eyes to the mosses aside
For a brief, little time; but they turn'd to the tide
In spite of his will, or of prayers well said.

He press'd four fingers against each lid,

Till the light was gone; yet for all that he did
It seem'd that the lithe forms lay and beat
Afloat in his face and full under his feet.

He seem'd to behold the billowy breast,
And the rounded limbs in their pure unrest—
To see them swim as the mermaid swims,
With the drifting, dimpled delicate limbs,
Folded and hidden or reach'd and caress'd.

It seems to me there is more that sees
Than the eyes in man; you may close your eyes,
You may turn your back, and may still be wise
In sacred and marvellous mysteries.
He saw as one sees the sun of a noon
In the sun-kiss'd south, when the eyes are closed—
He saw as one sees the bars of a moon
That fall through the boughs of the tropical trees,
When he lies at length, and is all composed,
And asleep in his hammock by the sundown seas.

He heard the waters beat, bubble and fret;
He lifted his eyes, yet forever they lay

Afloat in the tide; and he turn'd him away
And resolved to fly and for aye to forget.

He rose up strong, and he cross'd him twice,
He nerved his heart and he lifted his head,
He crush'd the treacherous reed in a trice,
With an angry foot, and he turn'd and fled.
Yet flying he hurriedly turn'd his head
With an eager glance, with meddlesome eyes,
As a woman will turn: and he saw arise
The beautiful Queen from the silvery bed.

She toss'd back her hair, and she turn'd her eyes
With all of their splendor to his as he fled;
Ay, all their glory, and a strange surprise,
And a sad reproach, and a world unsaid.

She beat on their shields, they rose in array,
As roused from a trance, and hurriedly came
From out of the wave. He wander'd away,
Still fretting his sensitive soul with blame,
Until all array'd; then ill and opprest,
And bitterly cursing the treacherous reed,
Return'd with his hand on his turbulent breast,
And struck to the heart, and most ill indeed.

* * * * *

Alone he would sit in the shadows at noon,
Alone he would sit by the waters at night;
Would sing sad-voiced, as a woman might,
With pale, kind face, to the pale, cold moon.

He would here advance, and would there retreat,
As a petulant child that has lost its way
In the redolent walks of a sultry day,
And wanders around with irresolute feet.

He made him a harp of mahogany wood,
He strung it well with the sounding strings
Of a strong bird's thews, and from ostrich wings,
And play'd and sang in a sad sweet rune.
He hang'd his harp in the vines, and stood
By the tide at night, in the palms at noon,
And lone as a ghost in the shadowy wood.

Then two grew sad, and alone sat she
By the great, strong stream, and she bow'd her head,
Then lifted her face to the tide and said,
"O, pure as a tear and as strong as a sea,
Yet tender to me as the touch of a dove,

I had rather sit sad and alone by thee,
Than to go and be glad, with a legion in love."

She sat some time at the wanderer's side
As the kingly water went wandering by;
And the two once look'd, and they knew not why,
Full sad in each other's eyes, and they sigh'd.

She courted the solitude under the rim
Of the trees that reach'd to the resolute stream,
And gazed in the waters as one in a dream,
Till her soul grew heavy and her eyes grew dim
To the fair delights of her own fair Isles.
She turn' her face to the stranger again,
He cheer'd with song and allured with smiles,
But cheer'd, andallured, and soothed in vain.

She bow'd her head with a beautiful grief
That grew from her pity; she forgot her arms,
And she made neglect of the battle alarms
That threaten'd the land; the banana's leaf
Made shelter; he lifted his harp again,

She sat, she listen'd intent and long,
Forgetting her care and forgetting her pain—
Made sad for the singer, made glad from his song.

* * * * * *

But the braves waxed cold; the white moons waned,
And the brown Queen marshall'd them never once more,
With sword and with shield, in the palms by the shore;
But they sat them down to repose, or remain'd
Apart and scatter'd in the tropic-leaf'd trees,
As sadden'd by song, or for loves delay'd
Or away in the Isle in couples they stray'd,
Not at all content in their Isles of peace.

They wander'd away to the lakes once more,
Or walk'd in the moon, or they sigh'd, or slept,
Or they sat in pairs by the shadowy shore,
And silent song with the waters kept.

There was one who stood by the waters one eve,

With the stars on her hair, and the bars of
the moon
Broken up at her feet by the bountiful boon
Of extending old trees, who did questioning
grieve;

"The birds they go over us two and by two;
The mono is mated; his bride in the boughs
Sit nursing his babe, and his passionate vows
Of love, you may hear them the whole day
through.

"The lizard, the cayman, the white-tooth'd boar,
The serpents that glide in the sword-leaf'd
grass,
The beasts that abide or the birds that pass,
They are glad in their loves as the green-leaf'd
shore.

"There is nothing that is that can yield one bliss
Like an innocent love; the leaves have tongue
And the tides talk low in the reeds, and the
young
And the quick buds open their lips but for this.

"In the steep and the starry silences,
On the stormy levels of the limitless seas,
Or here in the deeps of the dark-brow'd trees,
There is nothing so much as a brave man's kiss.

"There is nothing so strong, in the stream, on the land,
In the valley of palms, on the pinnacled snow,
In the clouds of the gods, on the grasses below,
As the silk-soft touch of a baby's brown hand.

"It were better to sit and to spin on a stone
The whole year through with a babe at the knee,
With its brown hands reaching caressingly,
Than to sit in a girdle of gold and alone.

"It were better perhaps to be mothers of men,
And to murmur not much; there are clouds in the sun.
Can a woman undo what the gods have done?
Nay, the things must be as the things have been."

They wander'd well forth, some here and some there,
Unsatisfied some and irresolute all.
The sun was the same, the moonlight did fall
Rich-barr'd and refulgent; the stars were as fair
As ever were stars; the fruitful clouds cross'd
And the harvest fail'd not; yet the fair Isle grew
As a prison to all, and they search'd on through
The magnificent shades as for things that were lost.

The minstrel, more pensive, went deep in the wood,
And oft-time delay'd him the whole day through,
As charm'd by the deeps, or the sad heart drew
Some solaces sweet from the solitude.

The singer forsook them at last, and the Queen
Came seldom then forth from the fierce deep wood,
And her warriors, dark-brow'd and bewildering stood

In bands by the wave in the complicate screen
Of overbent boughs. They would lean on their
spears
And would sometimes talk, low-voiced and
by twos,
As allured by longings they could not refuse,
And would sidewise look, as beset by their
fears.

Once, wearied and sad, by the shadowy trees
In the flush of the sun they sank to their
rests,
The dark hair veiling the beautiful breasts
That arose in billows, as mists veil seas.

Then away to the dream-world one and by one;
The great red sun in his purple was roll'd,
And red-wing'd birds and the birds of gold
Were above in the trees like the beams of the
sun.

Then the sun came down, with his ladders of
gold
Built up of his beams, and the souls arose
And ascended on these, and the fair repose
Of the negligent forms was a feast to behold.

The round brown limbs they were reach'd or
drawn,
The grass made dark with the fervour of hair;
And here were the rose-red lips and there
A flush'd breast rose like a sun at a dawn.

Then black-wing'd birds blew over in pair,
Listless and slow, as they call'd of the seas
And sounds came down through the tangle
of trees
As lost, and nestled, and hid in their hair.

They started disturb'd, they sprang as at war
To lance and to shield; but the dolorous
sound
Was gone from the wood; they gazed around
And saw but the birds, black-wing'd and afar.

They gazed at each other, then turn'd them
unheard,
Slow trailing their lances, in long single line;
They moved through the forest, all dark as
the sign
Of death that fell down from the ominous bird.

Then the great sun died, and a rose-red bloom

Grew over his grave in a border of gold,
And a cloud with a silver-white rim was roll'd
Like a cold grey stone at the door of his tomb.

* * * * *

Strange voices were heard, sad visions were
seen,
By sentries, betimes, on the opposite shore,
Where broad boughs bended their curtains of
green
Far over the wave with their tropical store.

A sentry bent low on her palms and she peer'd
Suspiciously through; and, heavens! a man,
Low-brow'd and wicked, look'd backward, and
jeer'd
And taunted right full in her face as he ran:

A low crooked man, with eyes like a bird,—
As round and as cunning,—who came from
the land
Of lakes, where the clouds lie low and at hand,
And the songs of the bent black swans are
heard;
Where men are most cunning and cruel withal,

And are famous as spies, and are supple and
fleet,
And are webb'd like the water-fowl under
the feet,
And they swim like the swans, and like pelicans
call.

And again, on a night when the moon she was
not,
A sentry saw stealing, as still as a dream,
A sudden canoe down the mid of the stream,
Like the dark boat of death, and as still as a
thought.

And lo! as it pass'd, from the prow there arose
A dreadful and gibbering, hairy old man,
Loud laughing as only a maniac can,
And shaking a lance at the land of his foes;
Then sudden it vanish'd, as still as it came,
Far down through the walls of the shadowy
wood,
And the great moon rose like a forest aflame,
All threat'ning, sullen, and red like blood.

PART V.

WELL, we have threaded through and through
The gloaming forests. Fairy Isles,
Afloat in sun and summer smiles,
As fallen stars in fields of blue;
Some futile wars with subtile love
That mortal never vanquish'd yet,
Some symphonies by angels set
In wave below, in bough above,
Were yours and mine; but here adieu.

And if it come to pass some days
That you grow weary, sad, and you
Lift up deep eyes from dusty ways
Of mart and moneys, to the blue
And pure cool waters, isle and vine,
And bathe you there, and then arise
Refresh'd by one fresh thought of mine,
I rest content: I kiss your eyes,
I kiss your hair, in my delight:
I kiss my hand, and say, "Good-night."

May love be thine by sun or moon,
May peace be thine by peaceful way
Through all the darling days of May,
Through all the genial days of June,
To golden days that die in smiles
Of sunset on the blessed Isles.

I TELL you that love is the bitterest sweet
That ever laid hold on the heart of a man;
A chain to the soul, and to cheer as ban,
And a bane to the brain and a snare to the feet.

Aye! who shall ascend on the hollow white wings
Of love but to fall; to fall and to learn,
Like a moth, or a man, that the lights lure to burn,
That the roses have thorns and the honey-bee stings?

I say to you surely that grief shall befall;
I lift you my finger, I caution you true,
And yet you go forward, laugh gaily, and you
Must learn for yourself, then mourn for us all.

You had better be drown'd than to love and to dream,
It were better to sit on a moss-grown stone,
And away from the sun, forever alone,
Slow pitching white pebbles at trout in the stream.

Alas for a heart that is left forlorn!
  If you live you must love; if you love, regret—
It were better, perhaps, had you never been
    born,
  Or better, at least, you could well forget.

The clouds are above us and snowy and cold,
  And what is beyond but the steel grey sky,
  And the still far stars that twinkle and lie
Like the eyes of a love or delusions of gold!

Ah! who would ascend? The clouds are above.
  Aye! all things perish; to rise is to fall.
And alack for lovers, and alas for love,
  And alas that we ever were born at all.

The minstrel now stood by the border of wood,
But not now alone; with a resolute heart
  He reach'd his hand, like to one made strong,
  Forgot his silence and resumed his song,
And aroused his soul, and assumed his part
With a passionate will, in the palms where he
    stood.

"She is sweet as the breath of the Castile rose,
  She is warm to the heart as a world of wine,

And as rich to behold as the rose that grows
  With its red heart bent to the tide of the Rhine.

"I shall sip her lips as the brown bees sup
From the great gold heart of the buttercup!
  I shall live and love! I shall have my day,
  And die in my time, and who shall gainsay?
"What boots me the battles that I have fought
  With self for honor? My brave resolves?
  And who takes note? The soul dissolves
In a sea of love, and the lands are forgot.

"The march of men, and the drift of ships,
  The dreams of fame, and desires for gold,
  Shall go for aye, as a tale that is told,
Nor divide for a day my lips from her lips.

"And a knight shall rest, and none shall say
    nay,
  In a green Isle wash'd by an arm of the seas,
  And wall'd from the world by the white
    Andes;
For years are of age and can go their way."

* * * * * * *

A sentinel stood on the farthermost land,
And struck her shield, and her sword in hand,
She cried, " He comes with his silver spears,
With flint-tipp'd arrows and bended bows,
To take our blood, though we give him tears,
And to flood our Isle in a world of woes.

" He comes, O Queen of the sun-kiss'd Isle,
He comes as a wind comes, blown from the seas,
In a cloud of canoes, on the curling breeze,
With his shields of tortoise and of crocodile."

* * * * *

Sweeter than swans are a maiden's graces!
Sweeter than fruits are the kisses of morn!
Sweeter than babes is a love new-born,
But sweeter than all are a love's embraces.

The Queen was at peace. Her terms of surrender
To love, who knows? and who can defend her?
She slept at peace, and the sentry's warning
Could scarcely awaken the love-conquer'd Queen;

She slept at peace in the opaline
Hush and blush of that tropical morning;

And bound about by the twining glory,
Vine and trellis in the vernal morn,
As still and sweet as a babe new-born,
The brown Queen dream'd of the old new
story.

But hark! her sentry's passionate words,
The sound of shields, and the clash of swords!
And slow she came, her head on her breast,
And her two hands held as to plead for rest.

Where, O where, were the Juno graces?
Where, O where was the glance of Jove,
As the Queen crept forth from the sacred
places,
Hidden away in the heart of the grove?

They rallied around as of old,—they besought
her,
With swords to the sun and the sounding
shield,
To lead them again to the glorious field,

So sacred to Freedom; and, breathless, they
brought her
Her buckler and sword, and her armor all
bright
With a thousand gems enjewell'd in gold,
She lifted her head with the look of old,
An instant only; with all of her might
She sought to be strong and majestic again:
She bared them her arms and her ample
brown breast;
They lifted her armor, they strove to invest
Her form in armor, but they strove in vain;
It could close no more, but it clang'd on the
ground,
Like the fall of a knight, with an ominous sound,
And she shook her hair and she cried, "Alas!
That love should come and that life should pass;"
And she cried, "Alas! to be cursed . . . and
bless'd,
For the nights of love and noons of rest."

Her warriors wonder'd; they wander'd apart,
And trail'd their swords, and subdued their
eyes
To earth in sorrow and in hush'd surprise,
And forgot themselves in their pity of heart.

"O Isles of the sun," sang the blue-eyed youth.
"O Edens new-made and let down from above!
Be sacred to peace and to passionate love,
Made happy in peace and made holy with truth.

"O gardens of God, new-planted below!
Shall rivers be red? Shall day be as night?"
Then he stood in the wood with his face to the foe,
Apart with his buckler and sword for the fight.

But the fair Isle fill'd with the fierce invader;
They form'd on the strand, they lifted their spears,
Where never was man for years and for years,
And moved on the Queen. She lifted and laid her
Finger-tip to her lips. For O sweet
Was the song of love, to the sense new-born,
That the minstrel blew in the virgin morn,
Away where the trees and the soft sands meet.

The strong men lean'd and their shields let fall,
And slowly they moved with their trailing spears,

And heads bow'd down as if bent with years,
And an air of gentleness over them all.

The men grew glad as the song ascended,
They lean'd their lances against the palms,
They reach'd their arms as to reach for alms,
And the Amazons came—and their reign was ended.

They reach'd their arms to the arms extended,
Put by their swords, and no more seem'd sad,
But moved as the men moved, tall and splendid—
Mingled together, and were all made glad.

Then the Queen stood tall, as of old she had stood,
With her face to the sun and her breast to the foe;
Then moved like a King, unheeding and slow,
And aside to the singer in the fringe of the wood.

She led him forth, and she bade him sing:
Then bade him cease; and the gold of his hair
She touch'd with her hands; she embraced him there,
Then lifted her voice and proclaimed him King.

And the men made fond in their new-found loves
Cried, "King and Queen!" and again and again
Cried, "Long may they live, and long may they reign,
As true in their loves as the red-bill'd doves :

"Ay, long may they live, and long may they love,
And their blue-eyed babes with the years increase,
And we all have love, and we all have peace,
While the seas are below or the sun is above.

"Let the winds blow fair and the fruits be gold,
And the gods be gracious to King and to Queen,
While the tides are grey or the Isles are green,
Or the moons wax new, or the moons wane old!"

The tawny old crone here lays her stone
On the leaning grass and reaches a hand ;
The day like a beautiful dream has flown,
The curtains of night come down on the land,
And I dip to the oars ; but ere I go,
I tip her an extra bright pesos or so,
And I smile my thanks, for I think them due :
But, fairest of readers, now what think you ?

O THOU To-morrow! Mystery!
O day that ever runs before!
What has thine hidden hand in store
For mine, To-morrow, and for me?
O thou To-morrow! what hast thou
In store to make me bear the now?

O day in which we shall forget
The tangled troubles of to-day!
O day that laughs at duns, at debt!
O day of promises to pay!
O shelter from all present storm!
O day in which we shall reform!

O days of all days to reform!
Convenient day of promises!
Hold back the shadow of the storm.
Let not thy mystery be less,
O bless'd To-morrow! chiefest friend,
But lead us blindfold to the end.

THE IDEAL AND THE REAL.

PART I.

> "*And full these truths eternal*
> *O'er the yearning spirit steal,*
> *That the real is the ideal,*
> *And the ideal is the real.*"

SHE was damn'd with the dower of beauty, she
Had gold in shower by shoulder or brow.
Her feet!—why, her two blessed feet, so small,
They could nest in this hand. How queenly tall,
How gracious, how grand! She was all to me,—
My present, my past, my eternity!
She but lives in my dreams. I behold her now
By shoreless waters that flow'd like a sea
At her feet where I sat; her lips push'd out
In brave, warm welcome of dimple and pout!
'Twas æons agone. By that river that ran

All fathomless, echoless, limitless, on,
And shoreless, and peopled with never a man,
We met, soul to soul.... No land; yet I think
There were willows and lilies that lean'd to
drink.
The stars they were seal'd and the moons were
gone.
The wide shining circles that girdled that world,
They were distant and dim. And an incense
curl'd
In vapory folds from that river that ran
All shoreless, with never the presence of man.

How sensuous the night; how soft was the
sound
Of her voice on the night! How warm was her
breath
In that world that had never yet tasted of
death
Or forbidden sweet fruit!.... In that far pro-
found
We were camped on the edges of god-land. We
Were the people of Saturn. The watery fields,
The wide-wing'd, dolorous birds of the sea,
They acknowledged but us. Our brave battle
shields

Were my naked white palms; our food it was
love.
Our roof was the fresco of gold belts above.

How turn'd she to me where that wide river
ran,
With its lilies and willows and watery reeds,
And heeded as only your true love heeds!....
How tender she was, and how timid she was!
But a black-hoofed beast, with the head of a
man,
Stole down where she sat at my side, and began

To puff his tan cheeks, then to play, then to
pause,
With his double-reed pipe; then to play and to
play
As never played man since the world began,
And never shall play till the judgement day.

How he puff'd! how he play'd! Then adown
the dim shore,
This half-devil man, all hairy and black,
Did dance with his hoofs in the sand, looking
back

As his song died away....She turned never
more
Unto me after that. She rose, and she pass'd
Right on from my sight. Then I followed as
fast
As a true love could follow. But ever before
Like a spirit she fled. How vain and how far
Did I follow my beauty, red belt to white star!
Through foamy white sea, unto storm stricken
shore!

How long I did follow! My pent soul of fire
It did feed on itself. I fasted, I cried;
Was tempted by many. Yet still I denied
The touch of all things, and kept my desire...
I stood by the lion of St. Mark in that hour
Of Venice when gold of the sunset is roll'd
From cloud to cathedral, from turret to tower,
In matchless, magnificent garments of gold;
Then I knew she was near; yet I had not known
Her form or her face since the red stars were
sown.

We two had been parted—God pity us!—when
This world was unnamed and all heaven was dim;

We two had been parted far back on the rim
And the outermost border of heaven's red bars;
We two had been parted ere the meeting of
men,
Or God had set compass on spaces as yet;
We two had been parted ere God had once set
His finger to spinning the purple with stars,—
And now at the last in the golden fret
Of the sun of Venice, we two had met.

Where the lion of Venice, with brows a-frown,
With tossed mane tumbled, and teeth in air,
Looks out in his watch o'er the watery town,
With a paw half lifted, with claws half bare,
By the blue Adriatic, on the edge of the sea,—
I saw her. I knew her, but she knew not me.
I had found her at last! Why I, I had sail'd
The antipodes through, had sought, and had
hail'd
All flags; I had climbed where the storm clouds
curl'd,
And call'd o'er the awful arch'd domes of the
world.

I but saw her one moment, then fell back
abash'd,

And fill'd to the throat....Then turn'd me once more,
Thanking God in my soul, while the level sun flashed
Happy halos about her. . . . Her breast!— why, her breast
Was white as twin pillows that lure you to rest.
Her sloping limbs moved like to melodies told,
As she rose from the sea, and threw back the gold
Of her glorious hair, and set face to the shore. .
I knew her! I knew her, though we had not met
Since the red stars sang to the sun's first set!

How long I had sought her! I had hunger'd, nor ate
Of any sweet fruits. I had followed not one
Of all the fair glories grown under the sun.
I had sought only her. Yes, I knew well that she
Had come upon earth, and stood waiting for me
Somewhere by my way. But the pathways of Fate
They had led otherwhere; the round world round,

The far North seas and the near profound
Had fail'd me for aye. Now I stood by that sea
Where she bathed in her beauty, God, I and she!

I spake not, but caught at my breath; I did raise
My face to fair heaven to give God praise
That at last, ere the ending of Time, we have met,
Had touch'd upon earth at the same sweet place. . . .
Yea, we never had met since creation at all;
Never, since ages ere Adam's fall,
Had we two met in that hunger and fret
Where two feast as one, but had wander'd through space;
Through space, and through spheres, as some bird that hard fate
Gives a million glad Springs but never one mate.

Was it well with my love? Was she true? Was she brave
With virtue's own valor? Was she waiting for me?
Oh, how fared my love? Had she home? had she bread?

Had she known but the touch of the warm-
    temper'd wave?
Was she born upon earth with a crown on her
    head,
Or born, like myself, but a dreamer instead? . .
So long it had been! So long! Why, the sea—
That wrinkled and surly, old, time-temper'd
    slave—
Had been born, had his revels, grown wrinkled
    and hoar
Since I last saw my love on that uttermost
    shore.

Oh, how fared my love? Once I lifted my face,
And I shook back my hair and look'd out on
    the sea;
I press'd my hot palms as I stood in my place,
And I cried "Oh, I come like a king to your
    side
Though all hell intervene!" . . . "Hist! she
    may be a bride,
A mother at peace, with sweet babes on her
    knee!
A babe at her breast and a spouse at her side!—
Have I wander'd too long, and has Destiny

Set mortal between us ?" I buried my face
In my hands, and I moan'd as I stood in my
place.

'Twas her year to be young. She was tall, she
was fair—
Was she pure as the snow on the Alps over there?
'Twas her year to be young. She was queenly
and tall ;
And I felt she was true, as I lifted my face
And saw her press down her rich robe to its
place,
With a hand white and small as a babe's with a
doll.
And her feet !—why, her feet in the white shin-
ing sand
Were so small, 'twas a wonder the maiden could
stand.
Then she push'd back her hair with a round
hand that shone
And flash'd in the light with a white starry stone.

Then my love she is rich ! My love she is fair !
Is she pure as the snow on the Alps over there?
She is gorgeous with wealth ! "Thank God, she
has bread,"

I said to myself. Then I humbled my head
In gratitude deep. Then I question'd me where
Was her palace, her parents ? What name did
she bear ?
What mortal on earth came nearest her heart ?
Who touch'd the small hand till it thrill'd to a
smart?
'Twas her year to be young. She was proud,
she was fair—
Was she pure as the snow on the Alps over there?

She loosen'd her robe that was blue like the sea,
And silken and soft as a baby's new born.
And my heart it leap'd light as the sunlight at
morn
At the sight of my love in her proud purity,
As she rose like a Naiad half-robed from the
sea.
Then careless and calm as a queen can be,
She loosed and let fall all the raiment of blue,
As she drew a white robe in a melody
Of moving white limbs, while between the two,
Like a rift in a cloud, shone her fair form through.

Soon she turn'd, reach'd a hand ; then a tall gon-
dolier

Who had lean'd on his oar, like a long lifted
spear,
Shot sudden and swift and all silently,
And drew to her side as she turn'd from the tide.
It was odd, such a thing, and I counted it queer
That a princess like this, whether virgin or bride,
Should abide thus apart as she bathed in the
sea ;
And I shook back my hair, and so unsatisfied !
That I flutter'd the doves that were perch'd
close about,
As I strode up and down in dismay and in doubt.

Swift she stept in the boat on the borders of
night
As a goddess might stand on that far wonder-
land
Of eternal sweet life, which men mis-name
Death.
I turn'd to the sea, and I caught at my breath
As she sat in the boat, and her white baby hand
Held vestments of purple to her throat, snowy
white.
Then the gondola shot,—shot sharp from the
shore:

There was never the sound of a song or of oar,
But the doves hurried home in white clouds to
Saint Mark,
Where the brass horses plunged their high
manes in the dark.

Then I cried, cried: "Follow her! Follow her!
Fast!
Come, thrice double fare, if you follow her true
To her own palace door!" There was plashing
of oar
And rattle of rowlock. . . . I sat leaning low,
Looking far in the dark, peering out as we sped
With my soul all alert, bending down, leaning
so . . .
But only the oaths of the men as we pass'd,
When we jostled them sharp as we sudden shot
through
The watery town. Then a deep, distant roar—
The rattle of rowlock, the rush of the oar.

We rock'd and we rode: then the oars keeping
pace
Gave stroke for short stroke in the swift stormy
chase.

I lifted my face, and lo! far, fitfully
The heavens breathed lightning: it did lift and
fall
As if angels were parting God's curtains. Then
deep
And indolent-like, and as if half asleep,
As if half made angry to move at all,
The thunder moved. It confronted me.
It stood like an avalanche poised on a hill,
I saw its black brows. I heard it stand still.

The pent sea throbb'd as if rack'd with pain.
Then the black clouds rose and suddenly rode,
As a fiery rider that knows no rein,
Right into the town. Then the thunder strode
As a giant striding from star unto star,
Then turn'd upon earth and frantically came,
Shaking the hollow heaven. And far
And near red lightning in ribbon and skein
Did seam and furrow the cloud with flame,
And write upon heaven Jehovah's name.

Then lightnings came weaving like shuttle-
cocks,
Weaving black raiment out of clouds for death.

The doves have swept to Saint Marco in flocks,
And mantled men hied them with gather'd
breath.
Black gondolas gathered as never before,
And drew like crocodiles up on the shore;
And vessels at sea stood further at sea,
And seamen haul'd with a bended knee,
And canvas came down to left and to right,
Till ships stood stripp'd as if stripp'd for fight!

Yet on! on! on where a huge house loomed
With its four walls wash'd by the foamy sea;
'Twas the place where Shelley once loved to be.
I heard in the heavens the howl of the doomed!
High up in the dark I did hear men shout;
And I lifted my eyes as the lightnings fell,
And I saw hands thrust through the bars; oh,
well
I knew 'twas the madhouse howling at me;
So doleful, so lorn! Like a land cast out,
And awful as Lucifer throned in hell.

Then an oath. Then a prayer. Then a gust
with rents
Through the yellow sail'd fishers. Then sud-
denly

Came sharp fork'd fire! Then again thunder
fell
Like the great first gun! Ah, then there was
rout
Of ships like the breaking of regiments,
And shouts as if hurled from an upper hell.
Then tempest! It lifted, it spun us about,
Then shot us ahead through the hills of the
sea
As if a steel arrow shot shoreward in wars—
Then the storm split open till I saw the blown
stars.

On! on! through the foam! through the storm!
through the town!
She was gone! She was lost in the wilderness
Of palaces, lifting their marbles of snow.
I stood in my gondola. Up and all down
We pushed through the surge of the salt-flood
street
Above and below. . . . 'Twas only the beat
Of the sea's sad heart. . . . Then I listened.
But oh,
'Twas the water-rat building, and nothing but
that;

Not even the sea-bird screaming distress,
As she lost her way in that wilderness.

I listen'd all night. I caught at each sound;
I clutch'd and I caught as a man that drown'd—
Only the sullen, low growl of the sea
Far out the flood-street at the edge of the
ships:
Only the billow slow licking his lips,
Like a dog that lay crouching there watching
for me—
Growling and showing white teeth all the night,
Reaching his neck and as ready to bite:
Only the waves with their salt-flood tears
Sad fawning white stones of a thousand years.

Only night birds in the loftiness
Of column and dome and of glittering spire
That thrust to heaven and held the fire
Of the thunder still; the bird's distress
As he struck his wings in that wilderness,
On marbles that speak, and thrill, and in-
spire.—
The night below and the night above;
The water-rat building, the startled white dove.

The wide-wing'd, dolorous, night-bird's call,
The water-rat building,—but that was all.

Silently, slowly, all up and all down,
I row'd and I row'd me for many an hour,
By beetling palace and toppling tower,
In the dark and the deep of the watery town.
Only the water-rat building by stealth,
Only the night-bird astray in his flight
As he struck his wings in the clouds of night,
On spires that sprang from old Adria's wealth;
On marbles that move with their eloquence,
On statues so sweeter than utterance.

Then, pushing the darkness from pillar to post,
The morning came sullen and grey like a ghost
Slow up the canal. I lean'd from the prow,
And listen'd. Not even the bird in distress
Screaming above through the wilderness;
Not even the stealthy old water-rat now.
Only the bell in the fisherman's tower,
Slow tolling at sea and telling the hour
To kneel to their sweet Santa Barbara
For tawny fishers at sea, and to pray.

PART II.

HIGH over my head, carved cornice, quaint spire.
And ancient built palaces knock'd their grey brows
Together and frown'd. Then slow-creeping scows
Scraped the walls on each side. Above me the fire
Of sudden-born morning came flaming in bars;
While up through the chasm I could count the stars.
Oh, pity! Such ruin! The dank smell of death
Crept up the canal: I could scarce take my breath!
'Twas the fit place for pirates, for women who keep
Contagion of body and soul where they sleep. . .

Great heavens! A white hand now beckon'd to me
From an old mouldy door, almost in my reach.

I sprang to the sill as one wrecked to a beach;
I sprang with wide arms: it was she! it was
she! . . .
And in such a damn'd place! And what was her
trade?
To think I had follow'd so faithful, so far
From eternity's brink, then from star to white
star,
To find her, to find her, nor wife nor sweet
maid!
To find her a shameless poor creature of shame,
A nameless, lost body, men hardly dared name.

All alone in her shame, on that damp dismal
floor
She stood to entice me. . . . I bow'd me before
All-conquering beauty. I call'd her my queen.
I told her my love as I proudly had told
My love had I found her as pure as pure gold.
I reach'd her my hand, as fearless a man
As man fronting cannon. I cried, "Hasten forth
To the sun! There are lands to the south, to
the north,
Anywhere you will. Dash the shame from
your brow;

Come with me, for ever; and come with me
now!"

Why, I had turn'd pirate for her! I had seen
Ships burn'd from the seas, like to stubble
from field.
Would I turn from her now? Why should I
now yield,
When she needed me most? Had I found her
a queen,
And beloved by the world,—why, what had I
done?
I had woo'd, and had woo'd, and had woo'd till
I won!
Then, if I had loved her with gold and fair
fame,
Would not I now love her, and love her the
same?
My soul hath a pride. I would tear out my
heart
And cast it to dogs, could it play a dog's part.

I told her all things. Her brow took a frown;
Her grand Titan beauty, so tall, so serene,
The one perfect woman, mine own idol queen—

Her proud swelling bosom, it broke up and
down
As she spake, and she shook in her soul as she
said,
With her small hands held to her bent, aching
head:
"Go back to the world! go back and alone!
You know naught of all; shame and death mine
own!"
I said: "I will wait! I will wait in the pass
Of death, until Time He shall break his glass .

"Don't you know me, my bride of the wide
worlds of zone?
Why, don't you remember the white milky-way
Of stars, that we traversed the æons before? . .
We were counting the colors, we were naming
the seas
Of the vaster ones. You remember the trees
That sway'd in the cloudy white heavens, and
bore
Bright crystals of sweets, and the sweet manna-
dew?
Why, you smile as you weep, you remember,
and you,

You know me! You know me! You know me!
    Yea,
You know me as if 'twere but yesterday!

"Now, here in the lands where the gods did
    love,
Where the white Europa was won,—she rode
Her milk-white bull through these same warm
    seas,-
Yes, here in the land where the Hercules,
With the lion's heart and the heart of the dove,
Did walk in his naked great strength, and strode
In the sensuous air with his lion's skin
Flapping and fretting his knotted thews;
Where Theseus did wander, and Jason cruise,—
Lo! here let the life of all lives begin.

"Yea! here where the Orient balms blow in,
Where heaven is kindest, where all God's blue
Seems a great gate open'd to welcome you,—
Come, rise and go forth, and forget your sin!"
Then outspake her great soul, so grander far
Than I had believed on that outermost star;
And she put by her tears, and calmly she said,
With hands enclasped and with bended head:

"I will go through the doors of death and wait
For you on the innermost side of the gate."

"It is breaking my heart; but 'tis best," she said.
"Thank God that this life is but a day's span,
But a wayside inn for woman, oh, man—
A night and a day; and, to-morrow, the spell
Of darkness is broken. Now, darling, farewell!
Nay, touch not the hem of my robe—it is red
With sins that your own sex heap'd on my head!
Now turn, yea turn! But remember I wait—
Remember, in sackcloth, I shall sit down and wait
Inside Death's door, and watch at the gate."

"Nay, nay," said I, "love! go patient on
through
The course that man hath compell'd you to;
Then come to your mother, the earth, my love;
Let press to her bosom your beautiful brow
Till it blends with her clay, and so purifies
Your flesh of the stains you say sully it now;
Lie down in the loam, the populous loam,
Yea, sleep but a day with death; then rise
As white, as light as the wings of a dove,—
And so made holy, oh love, come home!

"Farewell for a night! And now, oh my love
What thing on earth have I left to do?
Why, I shall sweep down through death's gate
as a dove,
And wait for your coming your swift day
through—
Your brave soul commanded, lo! I shall obey.
I shall sit, I shall wait for you, love, alway;
I shall wait by the side of the gate for you,
Waiting, and counting the days as I wait,
Yea, wait as that beggar that sat by the gate
Of Jerusalem, waiting the Judgment Day."

O TERRIBLE lion of tame Saint Mark!
Tamed old lion with the tumbled mane
Tossed to the clouds and lost in the dark,
With high-held wings and tail-whipp'd back,
Foot on the Bible as if thy track
Led thee the lord of the desert again
Say, what of thy watch o'er the watery town?
Say, what of the worlds walking up and down?

O silent old monarch that tops Saint Mark,
That sat thy throne for a thousand years,
That lorded the deep that defied all men,—
Lo! I see visions at sea in the dark;
And I see something that shines like tears,
And I hear something that sounds like sighs,
And I hear something that sounds as when
A great soul suffers and sinks and dies.

A DOVE OF ST. MARK

The high-born, beautiful snow came down,
Silent and soft as the terrible feet
Of time on the mosses of ruins. Sweet
Was the Christmas time in the watery town.
'Twas a kind of carnival swell'd the sea
Of Venice that night, and canal and quay
Were alive with humanity. Man and maid,
Glad in their revel and masquerade,
Moved through the feathery snow in the night,
And shook black locks as they laugh'd outright.

From Santa Maggiore, and to and fro,
And ugly and black as if devils cast out,
Black streaks through the night in the soft,
white snow,
The steel-prow'd gondolas paddled about:
There was only the sound of the long oars' dip,
As the low moon sail'd up the sea like a ship
In a misty morn. Then the low moon rose,
Rose veil'd and vast, through the feathery
snows,

As a minstrel stept silent and sad from his boat,
His mantle held tight in his hand to his throat.

"Grim lion," said he, "grim guard of St. Mark,
Down under your wings on the edge of the sea
In the dim of the lamps, on the rim of the
dark,
Alone I sit down in your salt-flood town.
O King on your column, all sullenly,
Wrinkle your brows and tumble your mane!
But the spouse turns not to his bride again." . .
Like a signal light through the storm let down,
Then a far star fell through the dim profound .
A jewel that slipp'd God's hand to the ground.

The storm has blown over! Now up and then
down,
Alone and in couples, sweet women they pass,
Silent and dreamy, as if seen in a glass,
Half mask'd to the eyes, in their Adrian town,
Such women! It breaks one's heart to think.
Water! and never a drop to drink!
What types of Titian! What glory of hair!
How tall as the sisters of Saul! How fair!
Sweet flowers of flesh, and all blossoming,

As if 'twere in Eden, and in Eden's spring.
"They are talking aloud with all their eyes,
Yet passing me by with never one word.
O pouting sweet lips, do you know there are
lies
That are told with the eyes, and never once
heard
Above a heart's beat when the soul is stirr'd?
It is time to fly home, O doves of St. Mark!
Take boughs of the olive; bear these to your
ark,
And rest and be glad, for the seas and the skies
Of Venice are fair. . . . What! wouldn't
go home?
What! drifting, as drifting as the soil'd sea-
foam?

"And who then are you? You! you so fair!
Your sweet child-face is a rose half-blown,
Down under your black and abundant hair? . .
A child of the street, and unloved and alone!
Unloved; and alone?....There is something
then
Between us two that is not unlike!....
The strength and the purposes of men

Fall broken idols. We aim and strike
With high-born zeal and with proud intent.
Yet let life turn on some accident.....

" Nay, I'll not preach. Time's lessons pass
Like twilight's swallows. They chirp in their
flight,
And who takes heed of the wasting glass?
Night follows day, and day follows night,
And no thing rises on earth but to fall
Like leaves, with their lessons most sad and fit.
They are spread like a volume each year to all;
Yet men nor women learn aught of it,
Or after it all, but a weariness
Of soul and body and untold distress.

" Yea, sit sweet child, by my side, and we,
We will talk of the world. Nay, let my hand
Fall round your waist, and so, let your face
Fall down on my shoulder, and you shall be
My dream of sweet Italy. Here in this place,
Alone in the crowds of this old careless land,
I will mantle your form till the morn and then—
Why, I shall return to the world and to men,

And you, no whit stain'd for the one kind
word
And some eagles of gold, my sad night bird.

"Fear nothing from me, nay, never once fear.
The day, my darling, comes after the night.
The nights they were made to show the light
Of the stars in heaven, though the storms be
near.....
Do you see that figure of Fortune up there,
That tops the Dogana with toe a-tip
Of the great gold ball? Her scroll is a-trip
To the turning winds. She is light as the air.

"Well, trust to Fortune....Bread on the wave
Turns ever ashore to the hand that gave.
What am I? A poet—a lover of all
That is lovely to see. Nay, naught shall
befall....
Yes, I am a failure. I plot and I plan,
Give splendid advice to my fellow-man,
Yet ever fall short of achievement....Ah me!
In my life's early, sad afternoon,
Say, what have I left but a rhyme or a rune.
A hand to reach to a soul at sea,

Or fair, to forbidden, sweet fruit to choose,
That 'twere sin to touch, and—sin to refuse?

"What! I to go home with you, girl, to-night?
To nestle you down and to call you love?
Well, that were a fancy! To feed a dove,
A poor, soil'd dove of this dear Saint Mark,
Too frighten'd for rest and too weary for flight.
Nay, nay, my sister; in spite of you,
Sister and tempter, I will be true....
Now here 'neath the lion, alone in the dark,
And side by side let us sit, my dear,
Breathing the beauty as an atmosphere....

"We will talk of your poets, of their tales of
love....
What! You cannot read? Why, you never
heard then
Of your Desdemona, nor the daring men
Who died for her love? My poor white dove
There's a story of Shylock would drive you wild.
What! never have heard of these stories, my
child?
Of Tasso, of Petrarch? Not the Bridge of
Sighs?
Not the tale of Ferrara? Nor the thousand
whys

That your Venice was ever adored above
All other fair lands for her stories of love?

"What then about Shylock? 'Twas gold. Yes—
dead.
The lady? 'Twas love....Why, yes; she too
Is dead. And Byron? 'Twas fame. Ah,
true....
Tasso and Petrarch? All died just the same....
Yea, so endeth all, as you truly have said....
And you, poor girl, are too wise; and you,
Too sudden and swift in your hard, hard youth,
Have stumbled face fronting an obstinate truth.
For whether for love, for gold, or for fame,
They but lived their day, and they died the
same.

"Let us talk not of death: of death, or the life
That comes after death. 'Tis beyond your
reach,
And this too much thought has a sense of
strife....
Ay, true; I promised you not to preach....
My maid of Venice, or maid unmade,
Lie still on my bosom. Be not afraid.

What! Say you are hungry? Well, let us dine
Till the near morn comes on the silver shine
Of the lamp-lit sea. At the dawn of day,
My pale child-woman, you can go your way.

What! You have a palace? I know your town;
Know every nook of it, left and right,
As well as yourself. For up and far down
Your salt-flood streets, lo! many a night,
I have row'd and have roved with a lady as fair
As the face of heaven. Nay, I know well there
Is no such a palace. What! you dare
To look in my face and to lie outright,
To bend your brows, and to frown me down?
There is no such place in that part of the town!

You would woo me away to your rickety boat!
You would pick my pockets! You would cut
my throat,
With help of your pirates! Then throw me out
Loaded with stones to sink me down,
Down into the filth and the dregs of your town!
Why, that is your damnable aim, no doubt!
And, beautiful child, you seem too fair,
Too young, for even a thought like that;

Too young for even black sin to dare—
Ay, even the devil to whisper at.

"Now, there is such a thing as being true
Even in villany. Listen to me:
Black-skinn'd women and low-brow'd men,
And desperate robbers and thieves; and then,
Why, there are the pirates!......Ay, pirates reform'd—
Pirates reform'd and unreform'd:
Pirates for me girl, friends for you,—
And these are your neighbors. And so you see
That I know your town, your neighbours: and I—
Well, pardon me, dear,—but I know you lie.

"Tut, tut, my beauty! What trickery now?
Why, tears through your hair on my hand like rain!
Come! look in my face: laugh, lie again
With your wonderful eyes. Lift up your brow,
Laugh in the face of the world, and lie!
Now, come! This lying is no new thing.
As well, ay, better, than you or I....
The wearers of laces know well how to lie.

But they lie for fortune, for fame: instead,
You, child of the street, only lie for your bread.

...."Some sounds blow in from the distant
land.
The bells strike sharp, and as out of tune,
Some sudden, short notes. To the east and afar,
And up from the sea, there is lifting a star
As large, my beautiful child, and as white
And as lovely to see as my lady's white hand.
The people have melted away with the night,
And not one gondola frets the lagoon.
See! Away to the land—'tis the face of morn.
Hear! Away to the sea—'tis the fisherman's
horn.

"'Tis morn in Venice! My child, adieu!
Arise, poor beauty, and go your way;
And as for myself, why, much like you,
I shall sell this story to who will pay
And dares to reckon it truthful and meet.
Yea, each of us traders, poor child of pain;
For each must barter for bread to eat
In a world of trade and an age of gain;
With just this difference, waif of the street,
You sell your body, I sell my brain.

"Poor lost little vessel, with never a keel.
Sore soul, what a wreck! Lo, here you reel,
With never a soul to advise or to care:
All cover'd with sin to the brows and hair,
You lie like a seaweed, well a-strand.
Blown like the sea-kelp hard on the shale,
A half-drown'd body, with never a hand
Reach'd out to help where you quiver and quail:
Left all alone so to starve and to lie,
And to sell your body to who may buy.

"My sister of sin, I will kiss you! Yea,
I will fold you and hold you close to my breast.
And as you lie resting in your first rest,
And as night is push'd back from the face of day,
I will push your heavy, dark heaven of hair
Well back from your brow, and kiss you where
Your ruffian, bearded, black men of crime
Have stung you and stain'd you a thousand time;
I call you my sister, sweet child, as you sleep,
And waken you not, lest you wake but to weep.

"Yea, tenderly kiss, and I shall not be

Ashamed, nor stain'd in the least, sweet
dove,—
I will tenderly kiss, with the kiss of Love,
And of Faith, and of Hope, and of Charity.
Nay, I shall be purer and be better then;
For, child of the street, you, living or dead,
Stain'd to the brows, are purer to me
Ten thousand times than the world of men,
Who reach you a hand but to lead you
astray.—
But the dawn is upon us! Rise, go your way.

"Here! take this money. Take it and say,
When you have well waken'd and I am away,
Roving the world and forgetful of you;
When you have aroused from your brief little
rest,
And find gold eagles nestled down in your
breast,
And rough men question you,—why, then say
That Madonna sent them. Then kneel and
pray,
And pray for me, the worst of the two:
Then God will bless you, sweet child, and I
Shall be the better when I come to die.

"You must keep this money and buy you bread,
And eat and rest while a year wears through.
Then, rising refresh'd, try virtue instead;
Be stronger and better, poor, pitiful dear,
So prompt with a lie, so prompt with a tear,
For the hand grows stronger as the heart grows
true....
Take courage, my child, for I promise you
We are judged by our chances of life and lot;
And your poor little soul may yet pass through
The eye of the needle, where laces shall not.

"Sad dove of the dust, with tear-wet wings,
Homeless and lone as the dove from its ark,—
Do you reckon yon angel that tops St. Mark,
That tops the tower, that tops the town,
If he knew us two, if he knew all things,
Would say, with your sins, you are worse than I?
Do you reckon yon angel, now looking down
And down like a star, he hangs so high,
Could tell which one were the worst of us two?
Child of the street—it is not you!

"If we two were dead, and laid side by side
Right here on the pavement, this very day,

Here under the lion and over the sea,
While the morn flows in like a rosy tide,
And the sweet Madonna that stands in the moon,
With her crown of stars, just across the lagoon,
Should come and should look upon you and
me,—
Do you reckon, my child, that she would decide
As men do decide and as women do say,
That you are so dreadful, and turn away?

"If God's angel were sent to choose this day
Between us two as we stand here,
Side by side in this storied place,—
If his angel were sent to choose, I say,
This very moment the best of the two,
You, white with a hunger and stain'd with a tear,
Or I, the rover the wide world through,
Restless and stormy as any sea,—
Looking us two right straight in the face,
Child of the street, he would not choose me.

"The fresh sun is falling on turret and tower,
The far sun is flashing on spire and dome,
The marbles of Venice are bursting to flower,
The marbles of Venice are flower and foam:

O child of the street, come turn you now!
There! bear my kiss on your beautiful brow
Through earth to heaven: and when we meet
Beyond the darkness, poor waif of the street,
Why, then I shall claim you, my sad, soiled dove;
Shall claim you, and kiss you, with the kiss of love."

IL CAPUCIN.

ONLY a basket for fruits or bread
 And the bits you divide with your dog, which you
Had left from your dinner. The round year through
He never once smiles. He bends his head
To the scorn of men. He gives the road
To the grave ass groaning beneath his load.
He is ever alone. Lo! never a hand
Is laid in his hand through the whole wide land,
Save when a man dies, and he shrives him home.
And that is the Capucin monk of Rome.

He coughs, he is hump'd, and he hobbles about
In sandals of wood. Then a hempen cord
Girdles his loathsome gown. Abhorr'd!
Ay, lonely, indeed, as a leper cast out.
One gown in three years! and—bah! how he smells!
He slept last night in his coffin of stone,
This monk that coughs, this skin and bone,

This living corpse from the damp, cold cells.—
Go ye where the Pincian, half-levell'd down,
Slopes slow to the south. These men in brown
Have a monkery there, quaint, builded of stone;
And, living or dead, 'tis the brown men's home,—
These dead brown monks that are living in
Rome!

You will hear wood sandals on the sanded floor;
A cough, then the lift of a latch, then the door
Groans open, and—horror! Four walls of stone
Are gorgeous with flowers and frescoes of bone!
There are bones in the corners and bones on
the wall;
And he barks like a dog that watches his bone,
This monk in brown from his bed of stone—
He barks, and he coughs, and that is all.
At last he will cough as if up from his cell;
Then strut with considerable pride about,
And lead through his blossoms of bone, and
smell
Their odors; then talk, as he points them out,
Of the virtues and deeds of the gents who wore
The respective bones but the year before.

Then he thaws at last, ere the bones are through,

And talks and talks as he turns them about
And stirs up a most unsavory smell;
Yea, talks of his brown dead brothers, till you
Wish them, as they are no doubt, in—well,
A very deep well....And that may be why,
As he shows you the door and bows good-bye,
That he bows so low for a franc or two,
To shrive their souls and to get them out—
These bony brown men who have their home,
Dead or alive, in their cells in Rome.

What good does he do in the world? Ah! well,
Now that is a puzzler....But, listen! He prays.
His life is the fast of the forty days.
He seeks the despised; he divides the bread
That he begg'd on his knees, does this old
shavehead.
And then, when the thief and the beggar fell!
And then, when the terrible plague came down,
Christ! how we cried to these men in brown
When other men fled! Who then was seen
Stand firm to the death but the Capucin?

SUNRISE IN VENICE.

NIGHT seems troubled and scarce asleep;
Her brows are gather'd in broken rest.
A star in the east starts up from the deep!
Tis morn, new-born, with a star on her breast,
White as my lilies that grow in the West!
Hist! men are passing me hurriedly.
I see the yellow, wide wings of a bark,
Sail silently over my morning-star.
I see men move in the moving dark,
Tall and silent as columns are;
Great, sinewy men that are good to see,
With hair push'd back, and with open breasts;
Barefooted fishermen, seeking their boats,
Brown as walnuts, and hairy as goats,—
Brave old water-dogs, wed to the sea,
First to their labors and last to their rests.

Ships are moving! I hear a horn,—
Answers back, and again it calls.
'Tis the sentinel boats that watch the town
All night, as mounting her watery walls,

And watching for pirate or smuggler. Down
Over the sea, and reaching away,
And against the east, a soft light falls,
Silvery soft as the mist of morn,
And I catch a breath like the breath of day.

The east is blossoming! Yea, a rose,
Vast as the heavens, soft as a kiss,
Sweet as the presence of woman is,
Rises and reaches, and widens and grows
Large and luminous up from the sea,
And out of the sea as a blossoming tree.
Richer and richer, so higher and higher,

Deeper and deeper it takes its hue;
Brighter and brighter it reaches through
The space of heaven to the place of stars.
Then beams reach upward as arms from a sea;
Then lances and arrows are aim'd at me.
Then lances and spangles and spars and bars
Are broken and shiver'd and strown on the sea;
And around and about me tower and spire
Start from the billows like tongues of fire.

A GARIBALDIAN'S STORY.

"AY, signor, that's Nervi, just under the lights
That look down from the forts on the Genoese heights;
And that stone set in stone in the rim of the sea,
Like a tall figure rising and reaching a hand,
Marks the spot where the Chief and his red-shirted band
Hoisted sail.... Have a light? Ah, yes! as for me
I have lights, and a leg—short a leg, as you see;
And have three fingers hewn from this strong sabre-hand.

"Look you there! Do you see where the blue bended floors
Of the heavens are fresco'd with stars? See the heights,
Then the bent hills beneath, where the grape-growers' doors
Open out and look down in a crescent of lights?

Well, there I was born; grew tall. Then the
call
For bold men for Sicily. I rose from the vines,
Shook back my long hair, look'd forth, then
let fall
My dull pruning-hook, and stood up in the
lines.
Then my young promised bride held her head
to her breast
As a sword trail'd the stones, and I strode
with a zest.
But a sable-crowl'd monk girt his gown, and
look'd down
With a leer in her face, as I turned from the
town.

"Then from yonder green hills bending down
to the seas,
Grouping here, grouping there, in the grey
olive trees,
We watch'd the slow sun; slow saw him retire
At last in the sea, like a vast isle of fire.
Then the Chief drew his sword: there was that
in his air,
As the care on his face came and went and
still came,

As he gazed out at sea, and yet gazed any-
where,
That meant more, signor, more than a peasant
can say.
Then at last, when the stars in the soft-
tempered breeze
Glow'd red and grew large, as if fann'd to a
flame,
Lo! something shot up from a black-muffled
ship
Deep asleep in the bay, like a star gone astray:
Then down, double quick, with the sword-hilt
a-trip,
Came the troop with a zest, and—that stone
tells the rest.

"Hot times at Marsala! and then under Rome
It was hell, sure enough, and a whole column
fell
Like new vines in a frost. Then year follow'd
year,
Until, stricken and sere, at last I came home—
As the strife lull'd a spell, came limping back
here—
Stealing back to my home, limping up out of
hell,

But we won, did we not? Won, I scarcely
know what—
Yet the whole land is free from the Alps to the
sea—
Ah! my young promised bride? Christ! that
cuts! Why, I thought
That her face had gone by, like a dream that
was not.

.... "Yes, peaches must ripen and show the
sun's red,
In their time, I suppose, like the full of a rose,
And some one must pluck them; that's very
well said,
As they swell and grow rich and look luscious
to touch:
Yet I fancy some men, some fiends, must have
much
To repent of: this reaching up rudely of hand
For the early sweet fruits of a warm, careless
land;
This plucking and biting of every sweet peach
Ere yet it be ripe and come well to its worth,
Then casting it down, and quite spoil'd, to the
reach

Of the swine and the things that creep close to
the earth....

"But he died! Look you here. Stand aside.
Yes, he died
Like a dog in a ditch. In that low battle-moat
He was found on a morn. The red line on his
throat
They said was a rope. 'Bah! the one-finger'd
man
Might have done it,' said one. Then I laugh'd
till I cried
When the guard led me forth, and the judge
sat to scan
My hands and my strength, and to question me
sore:
'Why, what has the match-man to do with all
this,—
The one-finger'd man, with his life gone amiss?'
I cried as I laugh'd, and they vex'd me no more.

* * * * *

"Some men must fill trenches. Ten thousand
go down
As unnamed and unknown as the stones in a
wall,

For the few to pass over and on to renown:
And I am of these. The old king has his crown,
And my country is free; and what more, after all,
Did I ask from the first? Don't you think that
yon lights
Through the black olive trees look divine on
the seas?
Then look you above, where the Appennines
bend:
Why, you scarcely can tell, as you peer through
the trees,
Where the great stars begin or the cottage-lights
end!

"Yes, a little bit lonely, that can't be denied:
But as good place to wait for a sign as may be.
I shall watch on the shore, looking out as before;
And the Chief on his isle in the calm middle sea,
With his sword gather'd up, stands waiting with
me
For the great silent ship. We shall cross to the
shore
Where a white city lies like yon Alps in the skies,
And look down on this sea; and right well
satisfied.

"Have a light, sir, to-night? Ah, thanks, signor,
thanks!
Bon voyage, bon voyage! Bless you and your
francs."

SIROCCO.

THERE were black clouds crossing the
Alps, and they
Roll'd straight upon Venice. Then far away,
As if catching new breath and gathering strength
In the Ægean hills, on the pall of the day,
Stood the terrible Thunder. Then hip and thigh

He smote all heaven, and the lightning leapt
Like red swords thrust through the Night full
length—
Ay! thrust through the black heart of Night as
he slept!
Then ribbon and skein kept threading the sky;
Then, ere you scarcely had time to think,
The sea lay darkling and black as ink.

Then many a sail, tri-colored, and cross'd
By the lone, sad cross of Calvary,

Drove by us and dwindled to blinding specks;
Drove straight in the grinning white teeth of
the sea,
Like lonesome spirits, forlorn and lost.
Then a ship with my stars of the West! and
then
There were golden crescents, tall turban'd men
All silent and devil-like, keeping the decks;
Then hearse-like gondolas hurried about,
As if sniffing the storm with their lifted snout.

COMO.

THE red-clad fishers row and creep
Below the crags, as half asleep,
Nor ever make a single sound.
The walls are steep,
The waves are deep;
And if a dead man should be found
By these same fishers in their round,
Why, who shall say but he was drown'd?

The lakes lay bright as bits of broken moon
Just newly set within the cloven earth;

The ripen'd fields drew round a golden girth
Far up the steeps, and glittered in the noon;
And when the sun fell down, from leafy shore
Fond lovers stole in pairs to ply the oar.
The stars, as large as lilies, fleck'd the blue;
From out the Alps the moon came wheeling
through
The rocky pass the great Napoleon knew.

A gala night it was,—the season's prime.
We rode from castled lake to festal town,
To fair Milan—my friend and I; rode down
By night, where grasses waved in rippled rhyme:
And so, what theme but love at such a time?
His proud lip curl'd the while with silent scorn
At thought of love; and then, as one forlorn,
He sigh'd; then bared his temples, dash'd with
grey;
Then mock'd, as one outworn and well *blase*.

A gorgeous tiger lily, flaming red,—
So full of battle, of the trumpet's blare,
Of old-time passion,—uprear'd its head.
I gallop'd past. I lean'd, I clutch'd it there
From out the long, strong grass. I held it high,

And cried: "Lo! this to-night shall deck her
hair
Through all the dance. And mark! the man
shall die
Who dares assault, for good or ill design,
The citadel where I shall set this sign."

O, she shone fairer than the summer star,
Or curl'd sweet moon in middle destiny;
More fair than sun-morn climbing up the sea,
Where all the loves of Adriana are....
Who loves, who truly loves, will stand aloof:
The noisy tongue makes most unholy proof
Of shallow passion....All the while afar
From out the dance I stood and watch'd my
star,
My tiger lily borne an oriflamme of war.

Adown the dance she moved with matchless
grace.
The world—my world—moved with her. Sud-
denly
I question'd whom her cavalier might be?
'Twas he! His face was leaning to her face!

I clutch'd my blade; I sprang; I caught my
breath,—
And so, stood leaning cold and still as death.
And they stood still. She blush'd, then reach'd
and tore
The lily as she pass'd, and down the floor
She strew'd its heart like jets of gushing gore..

'Twas *he* said heads, not hearts, were made to
break:
He taught me this that night in splendid scorn.
I learn'd too well....The dance was done. Ere
morn
We mounted—he and I—but no more spake....
And this for woman's love! My lily worn
In her dark hair in pride, to then be torn
And trampled on, for this bold stranger's
sake!....
Two men rode silent back toward the lake;
Two men rode silent down—but only one
Rode up at morn to meet the rising sun.

THE END.

www.ingramcontent.com/pod-product-compliance
Lightning Source LLC
LaVergne TN
LVHW010255110826
845151LV00004B/1474

* 9 7 8 1 4 2 5 5 2 1 9 0 5 *